Arctic Wars, Animal Rights, Endangered Peoples

Arctic Visions

Gail Osherenko and Oran Young,
General Editors

The Arctic has long appeared to outsiders as
a vast, forbidding wasteland or, alternatively,
as a storehouse of riches ready for the taking
by those able to conquer the harsh physical
environment. More recently, a competing vision paints the Arctic as the last pristine wilderness on earth, a place to be preserved for
future generations.

Arctic Visions confronts these conflicting and
simplistic portraits, conceived in ignorance
of the complexities of the circumpolar world
and without appreciation of the viewpoints
of those indigenous to the region. Drawing
upon an international community of writers
who are sensitive to the human dimensions,
Arctic Visions will explore political, strategic,
economic, environmental, historical, and cultural issues.

The Arctic has always been a place of human
and natural drama, an arena for imperial am-
bitions, economic exploitation, ecological di-
sasters, and personal glory. As the region
gains importance in international affairs, this
series will help a growing audience of readers
to develop new and more informed visions of
the Arctic.

*Arctic Politics: Conflict and Cooperation in the
Circumpolar North*, Oran Young, 1992

*Arctic Wars, Animal Rights, Endangered
Peoples*, Finn Lynge, 1992

FINN LYNGE

Arctic Wars • *Animal Rights*
• *Endangered Peoples* •

Translated by Marianne Stenbaek

Dartmouth College

Published by University Press of New England

Hanover and London

Dartmouth College
Published by University Press of New
England, Hanover, NH 03755
© 1992 by Finn Lynge
All rights reserved
Printed in the United States of America
5 4 3 2 1
CIP data appear at the end of the book

This material is based upon work supported by
the National Science Foundation under Grant
No. DPP-9100711. Any opinions, findings, and
conclusions or recommendations expressed in
this material are those of the author and do
not necessarily reflect the views of the National
Science Foundation.

We may be brothers after all. We shall see.
Chief Seattle, 1854

Contents

Foreword

This is a passionate book by a passionate advocate of environmental protection and the rights of indigenous people. We are fortunate to have, among the first offerings of the Arctic Visions series, a *Kalaallit* voice, a Greenlandic perspective on the Arctic.

Finn Lynge grew up in Greenland, the son of a Danish mother and a Greenlandic father. His insights emerge from a unique combination of life experiences—the first Catholic priest in his Lutheran country, social worker, radio station director, politician. Finn spent his novitiate in France, studied philosophy in Rome, and prepared for the priesthood in America. In the early 1980s, he served for five years as Greenland's representative to the European Parliament. In the mid-1980s, he worked for the Inuit Circumpolar Conference, a nongovernmental organization representing the interests of Inuit in Canada, Greenland, Russia, and the United States. At the ICC he initiated the world's first regional conservation strategy, a blueprint for economic growth and environmental protection of the Arctic region modeled after the World Conservation Strategy. From his current post as Greenland specialist in the Danish Foreign Ministry, Finn facilitates efforts to forge peaceful cooperation among Arctic states, and he participates in a multitude of other international fora on the global environment, human rights, and natural resources, including the International Whaling Commission.

The argument Finn Lynge presents here applies not only to the Arctic but to the world at large. By undervaluing indigenous cultures worldwide and depriving them of the right to use and manage the natural resources upon which they depend, dominant societies unwittingly disrupt not only the lives of indigenous peoples, but also nature. Animal rights advocates, in their insensitivity to indigenous people, may even destroy the animal species they set out to defend.

Unlike European and mainstream American cultures, indigenous peoples do not set themselves apart from (and over) animals and nature. Their dependency on animals for food, shelter, clothing, and transportation has not allowed the hubris common in civilizations that have adopted creation myths in which God creates man first and gives him dominion over all the earth. Such a view toward nature is hard to find among the world's remaining indigenous cultures, even among those that have adopted Christianity. Somehow, they have not entirely forgotten their earlier creation stories in which animals figure more prominently as the givers of life.

In *Arctic Wars*, Finn Lynge offers provocative insights derived from the biblical story of Jacob and Esau and from a well-known Alaskan myth, "The Whale's Soul and Its Burning Heart," brought back to Greenland by Knud Rasmussen in the 1920s. Thus the author confronts the questions of human/nature relations from both a Christian and an animistic perspective and underlines the difficult questions facing those of us who live more urbanized lives remote from the life-and-death realities of the hunter/gatherer. We hope that this work will narrow the gap in understanding what has led to human conflicts over seals, whales, and the trapping of wild animals.

January 1992   Gail Osherenko
                                                     Oran R. Young

Preface

This book was conceived in the corridors of the European Parliament in Strasbourg, France. As a member of Parliament for Greenland in the beginning of the eighties, I was taken aback by the stupendous emotional involvement of the public in the Newfoundland seal pup affair, a political uproar approaching that generated by famine in Africa or the war in Vietnam. Among the Inuit of the Arctic, seal hunters as they were, with no agricultural or industrial options, people were seized by bewilderment. What kind of phenomenon was this? they asked. Had they no right to be here?

Some years later, an American friend led me to Laurens van der Post's *A Mantis Carol*, a breathtaking account of the African bushmen's predicament and of the vantage point of Esau. Slowly it dawned on me that the shift in public attitudes toward nature, animals, hunting, and aboriginal life-styles is a global development.

We in the Arctic have been made to experience that development in a particularly poignant manner. The providers of our families have, for millennia and to this day, had no other choice than to put seal and whale meat on the dinner table and animal furs on the body. This book therefore deals with, first, the seal controversy that shook the very foundations of the Arctic cultures; then the protectionists who want the eaters of whale meat to change their ways and bow to the new taboos; and third, the swell of humane-society attitudes that want us all to walk around clad in nylon and polyester, do no harm to nature, and cause no death to any animal.

It is my contention that these movements are indicative of a growing alienation from the realities of nature and that they are—for a number of reasons—unsustainable in the long run.

In all fairness, it is time that people of the Arctic be heard. Their concern is legitimate and timely, and it reaches well beyond the regions of ice and snow. As a matter of fact, it is completely consistent with global concerns forwarded by the widely acclaimed Brundtland Commission Report and the World Conservation Union's *Caring for the Earth*: it is a matter of upholding the basic soundness of mankind's relation with the wild nature that we all want to protect.

This book does not pretend to do justice to the vast spectrum of questions raised about the contemporary relationship between animals and humans in the Arctic. A number of related fields are not mentioned at all, such as, for example, the intricate and very special situation in Alaska, where the native corporations are facing the termination of the Alaska Native Claims Settlement Act, or the enormous problems facing the formerly Soviet Arctic. So, too, will the reader look in vain for information about the lobbying at the Washington Convention's meetings about trade in products from endangered species; about the special regime pursuant to the Oslo Convention of 1973 allowing the aboriginal people of the Arctic a certain sustainable polar bear hunt; about the emerging environmental strategy of the Inuit Circumpolar Conference, the Canadian Northwest Territories, and the Yukon, or Greenland Home Rule's quite advanced natural resource management program; about the interesting propaganda techniques used by the World Society for the Protection of Animals, which functions as a global umbrella organization for 360 animal protection organizations in 66 countries; or about the work of the International Union for the Conservation of Nature and Natural Resources, the umbrella association of nature organizations and environmental ministries around the world, which has its own problems striking the proper balance between animal welfare pressure groups on the one hand and the protection of nature on the other.

This book would never have appeared in English but for the persistent interest and support offered by Professors Oran Young and Gail Osherenko of the Institute of Arctic Studies in Hanover, New Hampshire. For that assistance, I am more than thankful. They have provided the message expressed here with a sounding board it would otherwise never have gained.

Many friends in Denmark, Greenland, Canada, and Alaska have helped me with insights and information. Alan Herscovici of Montreal in particular has provided invaluable support, ever since the reading of his *Second Nature* prompted me to discuss the Greenland experience with him.

My thanks also go to Richard Caulfield for the use of his photographs and to those Gwich'in and Inupiat people in Alaska who gave permission to include certain of these photographs in this book.

A special word of thanks has to be addressed to the translator from the Danish, Professor Marianne Stenbaek of McGill University, Montreal, whose comments and encouragement have helped me mold the text for a North American public.

Most of all, inspiration has come to me from my friends in the Inuit Circumpolar Conference and Indigenous Survival International. This book is dedicated to their cause.

Abbreviations

ALF	Animal Liberation Front
APFA	Association for the Protection of Fur-Bearing Animals
API	Animal Protection Institute of America
CAHT	Canadian Association for Humane Trapping
CARC	Canadian Arctic Resources Committee
CBC	Canadian Broadcasting Company
EEC	European Economic Community
FIC	Fur Institute of Canada
FLA	Front pour la libération des animaux
FOA	Friends of Animals
FPCHT	Federal-Provincial Committee for Humane Trapping
HSUS	Humane Society of the United States
ICC	Inuit Circumpolar Conference
ICES	International Council for the Exploration of the Sea
ICNAF	International Commission for the Northwest Atlantic Fisheries
IFAW	International Fund for Animal Welfare
ILO	International Labor Organization
ISI	Indigenous Survival International
ISO-TC 191	International Standardization Organization Technical Committee 191
IUCN	International Union for the Conservation of Nature and Natural Resources
IWC	International Whaling Commission
IWGIA	International Work Group for Indigenous Affairs
MACOS	"Man: A Course of Study"
NAPO	North Atlantic Peace Organization
NASCO	North Atlantic Salmon Convention
NATO	North Atlantic Treaty Organization
PCBs	Polychlorinated biphenyls
UNCED	United Nations Conference on Environment and Development
UNEP	United Nations Environment Programme
WWF	World Wide Fund for Nature (formerly World Wildlife Foundation)

*Arctic Wars, Animal Rights,
Endangered Peoples*

I ✦ *A Way of Life*

If we look back over the horizon of time and observe the human race as it grows out of the mists of prehistory, one thing is certain: humanity appears as a link in the great biological machinery in which all parts, in one way or another, are interdependent. We are part of the biosphere, or, if you wish, of life on earth, plant life as well as animal life. Our ancestors have always gathered, harvested, and killed in order to eat. Even in death, we serve Mother Nature as food for worms. Humans are part of a circle that connects and reconnects.

This is a basic fact that nobody wants to challenge, but it is also a fact that humans, these omnivorous mammals endowed with both the molars of the plant-eaters and the incisors of carnivores, have brains producing phenomena otherwise unknown in the animal kingdom, namely, moral judgment and ethical imperatives: *coulds*, *shoulds*, and *oughts*. It is surprising to observe the extent to which these nebulous and intangible yet quite effective phenomena have managed to form and still create the history of humankind.

This ability and inclination to make moral judgments is now taking a direction unprecedented in history. In modern times a whole new subspecies of *Homo sapiens* has appeared, a product of the urban and industrial society that experiences its fundamental dependence on the biosphere as something embarrassing, inferior, even immoral. Nowadays we are often told that it is undignified for a human being to kill wild animals and eat them.

How in the world have we reached this stage?

First, the urban person has become alienated from nature and like everyone else fears the unknown. Therefore the city dweller shuns the sight of the predator feeding off its prey and abhors the smell of bleeding innards. The urbanite wants to see the meat neatly wrapped in plastic at the supermarket counter and, of course, appetizingly served on the dinner table. Certainly it is in bad taste to talk about how the meat got to the dinner plate.

Second, hunting and killing animals means inflicting physical pain on them, but urban people believe that pain ought to have no place in life. The gospel of the industrial and urban society is that you can have a shot of morphine for every broken leg, an aspirin for every headache, and a tranquilizer for every broken marriage. To inflict pain knowingly and willingly is immoral and undignified. It is a sin.

The hunter in the wilderness looks at this matter in a completely different way. Physical pain is part of life and always has been for every living creature. Birth is painful, death is painful, and few things in between are not painful in some way. Humans have toiled, hunted, traveled, begotten children, and wrestled with climate, illness and old age for untold hundreds of thousands of years without pain-killers and tranquilizers. It is very strange for the Indian trapper in the Canadian forests or for the Greenlandic seal hunter in a kayak—people who still live as their forebears did further back in history than anyone can remember—to hear comments made about the suffering of the poor animals. Who cares about the suffering that the hunter and the trapper themselves endure in order to secure the daily food for their families? All living things suffer; it has always been this way. Suffering is the price of life, and life feeds on death. Have the city dwellers forgotten this truth of life?

The third obvious comment is that for the ever-decreasing number of aboriginal hunters and trappers around the globe, the urban world appears to be a formidable adversary representing an overwhelming superpower of money, media mastery, and above all sheer numbers. How can the aboriginal hunters and trappers ever hope to have their voices heard and their viewpoint understood across this immense gulf of cultural alienation, misinformation, and plain ignorance?

The common denominator in this matter seems to be the question of respect for our fellow human beings. Everybody agrees, in principle, that we should respect animals. But what does this respect consist of? Does it mean doing everything in our power to spare the animals from physical suffering? Does it mean no longer killing ani-

An Inuit hunter resetting his leg-hold trap after removing an arctic fox. Eskimo Point, N.W.T., December 1989. (Photo by Erik Sander, Uldum, Denmark)

mals in the wild? Does it mean humanizing (note the word!) indus-trialized meat production? Does it mean, maybe, that human beings should stop killing animals altogether and become vegetarians?

Or does it possibly mean that the old hunting ethos should be upheld, the ethos which dictates that the hunter must respect his prey as his brother and his bride, and which holds that the soul of the animal accepts as rightful the ending of its life when it is taken and consumed by a human being?

All of these attitudes are expressed today somewhere in the world. Would it not be best if all of them were allowed to continue to exist side by side? Would it not be beneficial if human beings showed *each other* enough respect to understand that these many attitudes are possible and that a multiplicity of attitudes even concerning animals is a value to be treasured?

The present reality, of course, is quite different. Divergences in attitudes lead to conflict.

In industrialized society, the previously unequivocal relationship with animals is in disarray. There are now a multitude of opinions. There are the weekend hunters who relieve their own stress on body and soul by going out to kill a few partridges for their families' pots. There are numerous animal industries for the benefit of those many people who dislike hunting for survival or sport but want meat on their table and fur garments on their shoulders. There are the animal-protection societies who are militantly opposed to sport hunting and who are in favor of increasingly humane treatment of what they view as slave animals on death row in cages, be it in the food, fur, or cosmetic industry or for medical research. Then there are movements of people who are against the commercialized use of animals in industrial production but who support traditional small-scale animal farming as well as aboriginal peoples' wildlife harvests as long as they don't threaten any species. Finally, there are the vegetarians, who have moral objections to any organized killing of animals, whether for food or for medical experimentation. At the end of the line, as the logical outcome of much of this thinking, there are the fruit-eaters (the "Fruitarian Network") for whom the only morally acceptable foods are fruit and grain, that is to say, nature's own array of food items readily available and unquestionably meant to be eaten.

Intertwined with these many attitudes, the last decade has seen the development of a number of ecological and environmental movements whose objectives are the safeguarding of threatened wildlife habitats, sustainable exploitation of natural resources, and the creation of national legislation and international agreements to ensure a healthy natural environment, even in the wild.

Just to make things even more complicated, experience seems to show that movements originally intended to be ecological in scope, that is, to deal with the mutual balance and sustainability of natural resources, tend to slide into animal-protection postures, even where no ecological issues are at stake. This shift contributes to blurred boundaries in the environmentalists' landscape: clear issues become unclear, and misinformation abounds like bacteria in an old cheese.

Unfortunately, as we all know, this often becomes a game with high political stakes, and as in all politics it very often contains obscure objectives, secret agendas, and unethical means. In many instances, there are also important capital- investment interests involved. The relationship between humans and animals is a delicate matter in many ways.

The issue here is that we must safeguard a way of life against destruction. There are still millions of people around the world who live this kind of life and treasure it, and to whom nobody can offer anything better. Their existence must not needlessly be sacrificed to urban civilization. It is simply a question of human rights.

It is also more than that. If we safeguard aboriginal peoples' hunting and trapping rights in the modern world, we can save large and important wildlife areas from the encroachments of urbanization, disturbance, and pollution. Everyone who knows something of these matters will agree that the most important threat to wild animals is the mercilessly increasing destruction of wildlife habitats. Maintain these natural habitats in their original state and the animals will be able to survive. Destroy these habitats and the animals will become extinct. The best way to maintain habitats in their natural state is without a doubt to safeguard the political and legal rights of the peoples who for centuries have lived in harmony with nature on these very lands. They have a vested and continuing interest in protecting every species of animal and making sure that not a single one becomes extinct.

If, on the other hand, we deny the indigenous peoples their right to harvest, hunt, fish, and trap on their ancestral lands—deny them the right to live the life of their ancestors, prohibit them from setting traps, deny them access to their own forests and waterways—what will happen? Will the animals actually have a better existence? Quite the opposite. Numerous examples from the Amazon, Canada, and Alaska show us what is likely to happen. Industries will encroach on the large territories; forests will be cut down, mining towns will be erected; road systems will be built through the wild; enormous areas will be flooded with water by hydro-electric projects. Birds' nesting grounds will be disturbed; migration routes of the caribou and other wildlife will be diverted. The animals will be frightened by low-flying military training flights, here in the wild where pilots can do whatever they please because aboriginal hunters' rights are not respected.

Out of this maze of conflicts, one paradox stands out: in their struggle to make their age-old symbiosis with nature survive in a modern world, the hunter-gatherers of the upcoming millennium will have their most important allies in the midst of the enemy camp. The fact is that many practical and genuine nature lovers in the big cities and industrialized suburbia do support aboriginal peoples' land rights and do defend the right of the Indians and the Inuit to

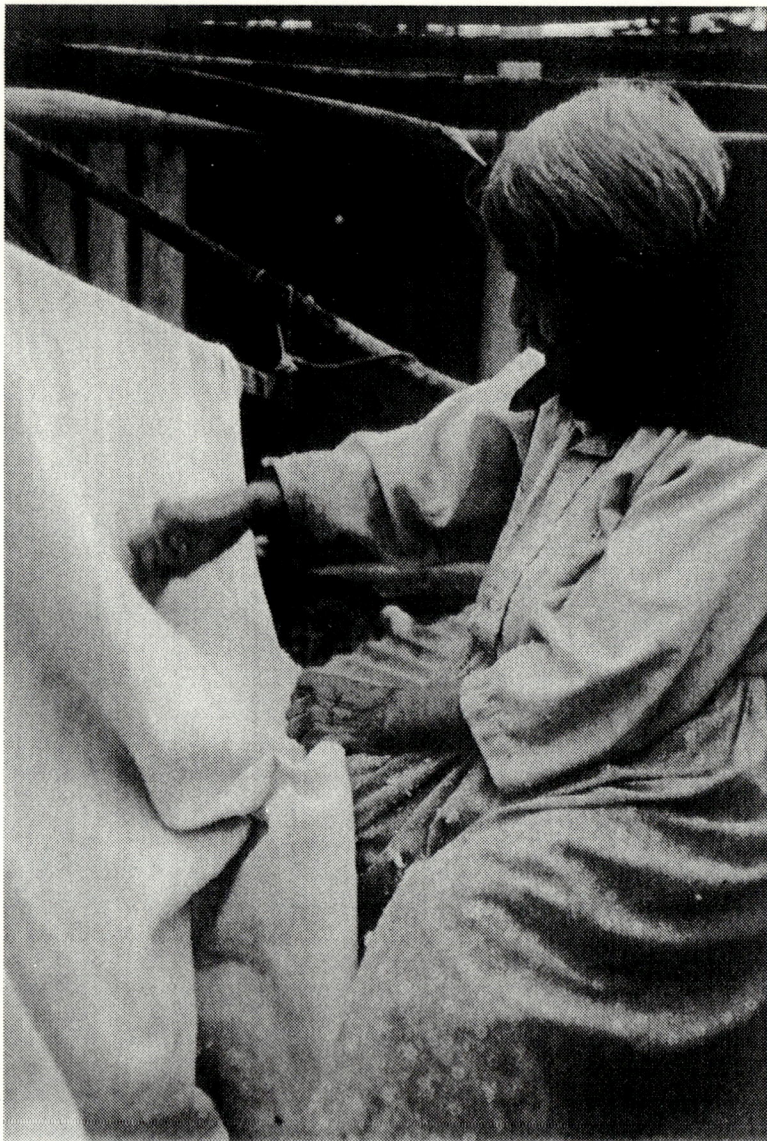

The late Grandma Sarah Frank of Venetie, Alaska, tanning moosehide. (Photo by Richard A. Caulfield, Fairbanks, Alaska)

In northern Quebec, many thousands of caribou have drowned in the artificial lakes and streams generated by the great hydroelectric projects. The migration routes of the caribou are severed. Caniapiscau River, northern Quebec, 1984. (From Gail Osherenko and Oran Young, *The Age of the Arctic: Hot Conflicts and Cold Realities*, Cambridge University Press, 1989)

hunt and market their products. They do understand that in their efforts to stop the global onslaught on nature and its animal life, in their deep desire to hand over to their grandchildren a world of beauty, life, and respect for everything living, they have no better allies than the indigenous hunters and fishermen who live on their ancestors' land.

The ongoing debate concerning the proper use versus nonuse of nature is not a pleasant one. Aside from all the political and economic interests involved, because of the emotion involved the exchange of views often takes place in a near-fanatic mode quite different from most other public debates. People in big cities have little or no personal experience of nature, yet many do feel a strong urge to help save what is threatened. So, having no experience, they may compensate by choosing sides, the mechanism apparently being that the less they know through individual and personal contact with animals in the wild, the more uncompromisingly black-and-white are the stances they take against anybody setting a trap in the woods or wielding a weapon on the ice floes. And so there it is, for anyone to see: to the extent that intensity of commitment in a debate works as a substitute for personal encounter and experience, fanaticism lurks around the corner.

There is nothing wrong with taking sides in a debate, nothing wrong with the concept of personal involvement. But it is paramount that commitments be based on genuine experience and not just on "correct ideas" inculcated from either side. Where people's attitudes are woven from the living fabric of personal encounter and reflection, they may be at odds. But there will always be an opening for dialogue.

2 ♦ *The Seal War*

A hunter in a kayak with a lifted harpoon. A man slowly crawling over the ice floe, gun in hand. A woman with an ancestral ulu in her hands, flensing a seal on the beach. Yes, most people have pictures in their heads of the traditional Eskimo, with the seal at the center of his or her life. The seal is the hunter's prize, everyday food, clothing and footwear and—in the old days—light and heat.

This is the uncomfortable story of what has happened with this seal-hunting culture, not only in Canada but also among the Inuit in Greenland.[1] The story is familiar to many in Scandinavia, but it is still not widely known in Holland, in Great Britain, or in the United States. This culture has been pushed into a corner and sacrificed to forces it does not understand and by which it is not understood. It is the casualty of a war in which it has never wished to participate.

The Prologue

Like nearly all modern wars, this one had a slow and incremental start. There was no declaration of war but only sporadic and faraway conflicts that did not seem at first to have much to do with the Inuit sealers. The actuality turned out to be different.

Everything started, as so much in this world does, with something quite different, namely, the animal-protection societies in the large industrial nations of North America and Europe. In March 1977 they organized a media event that was to be of major importance. Brigitte Bardot—no introduction necessary—had decided to go to Newfoundland and observe the yearly mass hunt on seal pups. A picture of the beautiful actress cheek to cheek with a small white

Harbor seals on the ice. Southeast Alaska. (Photo by Richard A. Caulfield, Fairbanks, Alaska)

seal pup was shown by the media globally. It was a stroke of genius, just as it had been to refer to these young animal pups as *babies*. What every film maker knows and what every advertising person knows is that nothing sells better than beautiful women and cuddly little animals. In the Bardot picture a number of connotations came together in one image with strong undertones of sex, violence, and mother instinct mixed in. The picture appealed to men, women, and children around the world. If nobody had noticed the Newfoundland seal hunt before, now everybody did.

The Bardot story had its beginning in an invitation from a rich Swiss by the name of Franz Weber, who had declared that he wanted to travel over the ice near Newfoundland, bringing with him six hundred journalists and four hundred thousand dollars that he planned to use to pay the hunters to keep away from the animals. When he finally arrived in March, he brought along sixty journalists, no money—and Brigitte Bardot. There are different versions of what happened next. The original idea had been that Bardot should meet the well-known founder and leader of the International Fund for Animal Welfare (IFAW), Brian Davies, in the small town of Saint Anthony, and together with him fly out over the ice in a Greenpeace helicopter. But her flight was delayed, and Davies had had problems with the local population and had therefore gone ahead without her. So she had no choice but to turn back, without accomplishing her mission. A Newfoundland radio program reported that she therefore decided to go out on the ice with another Greenpeace group. However, they appeared to have gone in the wrong direction. She still saw no seals and was reported to have been quite angry about it.

Eventually, somehow or other, a seal pup was procured, and a photograph was taken of the famous actress with the animal in her arms. The picture went around the world with great effect. Discussions about the political necessity of reducing the Canadian seal pup hunt quotas got under way.

It may be too much to give Bardot all the honor—or blame—for this development. During these years much opposition was mobilized against the seal hunt. It slowly became a campaign of dimensions that had never been seen before. This campaign allowed a large number of nature- and animal-protection organizations to discover for the first time what potential they actually had, with regard both to public relations and to the economy. The IFAW, Greenpeace, the Animal Protection Institute of America (API), the Seal Rescue Fund, the Humane Society of the United States (HSUS), Friends of Animals (FOA), Sea Shepherd, and later numerous other organizations in Europe decided to pool their efforts to stop the seal pup hunt near Newfoundland.

Why?

In the very comprehensive debate, seven concerns were expressed openly by opponents of the hunt:

—the seal pup hunt is cruel;
—it is unnecessary;
—the seal species is endangered;
—the industrial hunt of seal pups is inappropriate;
—it is vanity and luxury to use seal fur;

—it is immoral to kill animals in the wild;
—it is particularly unethical to kill small pups.

There was an unexpressed but implicit additional charge:

—the seal pup hunt is equivalent to child murder.

Aside from these claims, stated and otherwise, there is good reason to conclude also that the antisealing campaigns

—are good business;
—contribute to distinguishing the protest organization in question as "environmentally concerned"—an important asset nowadays.

Now let us look at each of these elements in some detail.

The Cruelty

Seal hunting is cruel, just like any other hunt or butchery. Skulls are crushed by hundreds of thousands and blood flows in streams in authorized slaughterhouses all over Europe and North America. Livestock and poultry suffer fear and stress when they are transported to mass deaths by knife or stun gun. Birds suffer when they are filled with the hunter's lead pellets. The seals of the Arctic waters feel no special pleasure at getting harpoons stuck into their blubber. And the seal pup hunt off Newfoundland was a gruesome spectacle for anyone not used to that kind of sight.

That the Newfoundland seal pup hunt was *especially* cruel or gruesome is, however, not true. The crushing of the skull caused instantaneous death at the first hit. If the animal continued to move, it was because of the same reflexes that make a beheaded chicken run around in the yard and that make butchered cattle kick when they have been stunned by the stun gun. A seal pup's skull is fragile, and even though one blow would be sufficient, the Canadian veterinary legislation demanded several blows with this killing method.

That this method was especially bloody is also not true. A ten-day-old pup doesn't contain much blood. The stained ice floes appeared as they did on color television not only because of the mandatory exsanguination of the pups—an official veterinary regulation aimed at a quick and humane death for the animals—but also because of the blood from the mother seal when she gave birth. A bloody placenta lying around for weeks on ice and snow in the sunshine is striking to the eye. Why was this simple fact never conveyed by the television commentators?

There was only one aspect that separated this seal pup hunt from authorized industrial killing: it took place outdoors. It met the eye in an extraordinarily surprising and beautiful landscape of ocean and ice, a wavy scenery where the eye could not encompass the thousands of animals that moved over the ice floes and where the camera shocked us into disbelief and nausea when it registered the old, primordial color: red against white, blood on ice.

The public came to associate the Newfoundland hunt with cruelty and inhumanity first and foremost because of the television productions filmed there. In 1964 the Montreal production company Artek Film was hired by the provincial government in Quebec to produce a series of nature films. When the film crew returned from the ice near Newfoundland, they brought home with them some film sequences that were to go around the world and arouse antisealing sentiments of hitherto-unknown intensity. These film scenes depicted a man torturing a seal in different ways and then, at the end, skinning it alive.

This was proof, people thought. Images do not lie. This barbarian practice, they concluded, had to be stopped. A storm of outrage and protest arose everywhere the film was shown. Later, doubts were raised about the film. Was it authentic? The judicial system got involved, and it was demonstrated that two of the three men shown in the film were in fact members of the film crew. The third man was a certain Mr. Poirier, who gave the following testimony: "'I, the undersigned, Gustave A. Poirier, of the Magdalen Islands, declare having been employed by a group of photographers, one of which had a beard, around March 4, 1964, to skin a large seal for a film. I solemnly swear before witnesses that I was asked to torment the said seal and not to use a stick, but just to use a knife to carry out this operation, where in normal practice a stick is used to first kill the seals before skinning them'"[2]

In 1968 the Canadian Broadcasting Corporation (CBC) finally received a reprimand from the Federal Department of Fisheries for irresponsibility in not having investigated the authenticity of the film before it was broadcast over television. But nobody listened to this correction of error. It was too late. The entire world was now totally convinced that the seal hunt in Newfoundland was an extraordinarily barbaric event. People had seen it with their own eyes.

The Necessity

If you were to ask the fishermen in Newfoundland whether this hunt is necessary, they would answer a clear yes. If you were to ask members of the public in Europe and North America, they would answer no.

In Newfoundland they say yes for two reasons: wildlife management and economy.

If you do not remove approximately 150,000 seal pups from their birthplace every year, the population of seals will get out of control. Newfoundlanders think of the seal not only as a natural resource but also as a competitor. Every individual adult seal of this species, that is, the harp seal, is capable of eating approximately 7 pounds of fish a day. That represents 1¼ tons of fish every year. If we take into account that approximately one-third of the young ones die a natural death, that still leaves 100,000 seals who may eat around 125,000 tons of seafood each year—not necessarily the precise kind of fish the fishermen are interested in, but still 125,000 tons of biomass made unavailable. That quantity can be felt in the fisheries, which are the main source of income for the inhabitants here. To the Newfoundland fishermen, the conclusion is clear: the seal population has to be controlled. After all, farmers also control the population of deer in adjacent forests so that they don't ruin the harvest.

The seal pup hunt in the spring was a welcome economic stimulus after the winter's lack of employment and very low income. From the perspective of the Canadian taxpayer, not much money was involved. A Newfoundland fisherman used to estimate that if he worked hard, he would earn only a couple of thousand dollars during the four to six weeks of the seal pup hunt. Nevertheless, in many cases this made up almost a third of his yearly income. For an otherwise very poor and economically destitute fishing family, these very few dollars meant a great deal.

Newfoundlanders also like to eat seal meat. Although there is not much meat on the young pups, the seal flippers have always been looked upon as a great delicacy. It is not true that edible seal pup

From time immemorial, seals have been the mainstay of the Inuit diet, from Siberia in the East to Greenland in the West. The seal provides food and clothing, and until a few generations ago, also provided light and heat. Seal hunting has always been and remains household-oriented, not industrial. The Netsilingmiut, named after natseq, *the ringed seal, live in the eastern Canadian Arctic. The stocks are doing well, and the seals are unusually robust. Pelly Bay, N.W.T., July 1964* (Photo by the author)

meat was thrown away because of pure greed for the fur. It was a Newfoundland tradition to use the edible parts of the hunt as well.

Members of the public who saw the television broadcasts believed that this hunt was unnecessary. The principle of wild life management did not mean anything to urban TV viewers, because they thought, and continue to think, that nature should be allowed to regulate itself. But the fact is that these people know nothing about the consequences of such self-regulation. That the fisherman also has the right to live off the ocean and to defend its resources, the general public does not understand. The economic advantage gained from the seal pup hunt was so relatively small that people really ought to be able to get by without it, said the nature lovers who had nothing to lose themselves. It really did not mean that much to them if these poor people lived even more poorly, as long as they just stopped what they were doing to the baby seals!

The Threat of Extinction

The seal in question is the harp seal or the Greenland seal (*Phoca groenlandica*), the latter name given because the animal was first seen by Europeans in great numbers near the coast of Greenland. That its name is officially related to Greenland is the main reason for an understandable, but to the Greenlanders an almost catastrophic, misunderstanding. Thousands of people have been lead to believe that Greenland is the seals' only home, although precisely this seal species does not breed in Greenland at all.

The harp seal is not an endangered species and never has been. It breeds by the millions in three well-demarcated areas near Newfoundland, in Jan Mayen, and in the Beljoe More (The White Sea) and spends the summer and the fall in the incredibly large Arctic archipelago in Canada, along the coast of Greenland, near Iceland and Spitzberg, and in the Norwegian Sea and the Barents Sea.

Of course, even if a species is not threatened with extinction, a particular stock within that species can be quite vulnerable. It has rightly been said that this is so with the stock that breeds near Newfoundland and from there spreads toward the north into the Canadian Arctic waters and to the west of Greenland. The reason this seal population was endangered at one time was that others besides the Newfoundland fishermen were using these animals. They had come to be exploited industrially on a large scale.

The industrialized seal hunt dates back to the end of the eighteenth century, and by the period from 1830 to 1850, the average catch was 450,000 animals every year. This figure decreased in the following seventy-five years to around 150,000, but increased thereafter until in 1955 it had reached 350,000 per year. The increase in the seal harvest during the twentieth century resulted to some extent from the fact that in the 1930s, Norwegian steel ships were able for the first time to break through the ice everywhere and thus reach breeding grounds that had never before been exploited.

At that time, as for centuries before, the seal was still hunted for its blubber. These ships, and subsequent ships in the years after the

Second World War, were equipped rationally and effectively for the hunt. They were operated with freezer compartments so that in addition to the blubber, which was the main reason for the hunt, the beautiful fur of the young seal pups could also be taken without damage to it. The Norwegian industrial seal hunt was a model for the Canadians, who then started to join it. At the same time the market began to decrease its demand for the once-valuable blubber but increased its demand for the pelts of the young seal pups, the so-called whitecoats.

Then everything started to move quickly.

In 1949, the year Newfoundland joined the Canadian confederation, the first scientific group was established to study the seal population. In 1952 it became, for the first time, more lucrative to hunt the seals for their pelts than for their blubber. But in the mid-1950s the first protests were heard. In 1961 twenty-eight ships participated in the seal hunt, with radar, airplanes, and the assistance of icebreakers. An attempt was made to include the seal hunt under the auspices of the International Commission for Northwest Atlantic Fisheries (ICNAF), a multinational scientific advisory organization, though without success.[3] In 1962 helicopters were incorporated into the seal hunt, and the helicopter operators were accused of stealing faraway pelt depots from the sailors. The Russians arrived in that year with a seven-thousand-ton icebreaking seal-hunt ship with two immense helicopters.

The peak year for the seal hunt was 1964. One hundred and fifty airplanes and helicopters took part in the hunt that year. Many inexperienced men were sent out on the ice. Many seals were killed without being used or being transported away from the site. Later on it was estimated that the population had been reduced to 1.5 million, decimated by 200,000 animals since 1950, and probably halved during the last hundred years. It became clear that things were moving in the wrong direction, and probably had been doing so for a number of years.

The 1964 hunt season had been chaotic, and the hunt could not continue in this manner. New regulations shortened the hunting season. The hunters had to have a hunt permit in order to gain admission to the ice, and the number of airplanes used to locate the large concentrations in the population were limited. Veterinary authorities regulated the kinds of bats that could be used to club the seals.

The usual practice of killing the animals before skinning them became formalized by law, and a quota of 50,000 pups was set in the Saint Lawrence Bay (which was inside Canadian jurisdiction, although a large part of the hunt took place outside).

It took some years before the authorities succeeded in controlling the situation, but eventually the population decline turned around. Estimates from the biologists became more accurate. The veterinary authorities and the police exercised a tighter control. There was also escalating interest in international cooperation concerning a constructive solution to the problems at hand.

Already in 1966 ICNAF had established a special "seal panel," and in 1971 a bilateral Norwegian-Canadian seal commission was set up. This resulted in 1971 in a quota of 245,000 animals near Newfoundland. In 1972 the number was reduced to 150,000, three-quarters of which could be the coveted whitecoats.

In 1972 a quota effective outside the territorial limits was agreed upon, and from 1976 on, the seal commission stabilized the catch limit at 170,000 animals per year. The situation was now under control; that is, the future of the stock population was no longer in danger. On the contrary, the Newfoundland seal population was undergoing a slow and controlled growth.

Why then did the public, in the following years, continue to be given the impression that the seal population was being decimated and that the harp seal was in danger?

Why couldn't the media become interested in the serious scientific data that were now available?

Why did the environmental movement continue to push the matter for another ten years, even though no one could seriously claim that this was an *ecological* matter? That the animal-protection organizations continued to protest is possibly understandable, but why the *environmental* organizations?

Why was almost no effort made to save the only seal species that really was (and is) threatened with extinction, namely, the monk seal in the Mediterranean? Why were everyone's eyes turned toward the nonthreatened seal pups near Newfoundland, by all now called *babies*, and not toward the endangered species near the Greek and Italian coasts?

Nature protection had arrived at a crossroad, and the signposts pointed in a new direction. With emotions running higher than ever, thinking on the issue became muddy.

Appropriateness

A large part of the public mood that was whipped into a frenzy against the seal pup hunt near Newfoundland I think has to be called misinformed and hysterical. But the Inuit posed themselves at least one reasonable question during these years, and that was whether this hunting method really was a suitable use of the resource. The meat that could be harvested from each tiny animal was minimal. One would get a much larger harvest of nature's gift by letting the seals grow big and fat before killing them for their pelts *and* for their meat.

In this form of analysis, two hunting cultures confront each other: on the one side, the aboriginal subsistence hunt, which is household-oriented and in which the hunter goes after the prey with the most meat, and all parts of the animal are used; on the other side, the modern industrial hunt, which is directed exclusively toward one specific and economically valued part of the animal, with the rest thrown away.

By and large, the Inuit did not get themselves involved in the battle of Newfoundland. In Greenland particularly, the public opinion was—quite wrongly—that Canada was so far away and the hunt in question so un-Inuit that nobody in Greenland would be touched by this dispute. If a public opinion poll had been taken in Greenland in the seventies concerning the seal pup hunt near Newfoundland, the result would probably have shown among most Inuit a certain sympathy for the local fishermen, who managed to get through a meager season by taking a modest number of seal pups given to them by nature's abundance where they lived. However, the poll would also have shown that Inuit reacted very strongly against the industrial butchery, which seemed to threaten the existence of an entire breeding ground and which—at least for a time—did not seem capable of controlling itself and creating its own limits.

From the perspective of a wise and rational use of a hunting ground, the industrial seal pup hunt was neither appropriate nor desirable.

Vanity and Luxury

If the behavioral patterns of people through the centuries are divided into two cultures, a fur culture and an antifur culture, then it can be said that the first has dominated almost everywhere until the middle of this century. Ever since the Stone Age, through the Bronze Age and the Iron Age and up to our own days, large numbers of people all over the world have dressed themselves in skins and fur as the only natural and, in some areas, the only available materials. Even in those cultures where textiles became dominant, fur remained important. The nobles wore sable and marten; the kings were dressed in ermine. Even today in our industrial society, we have inherited the notion that beautiful fur is prestige apparel.

At present, when the fur hunt culture has turned a corner and suddenly sees itself becoming an object of hatred, we are experienc-

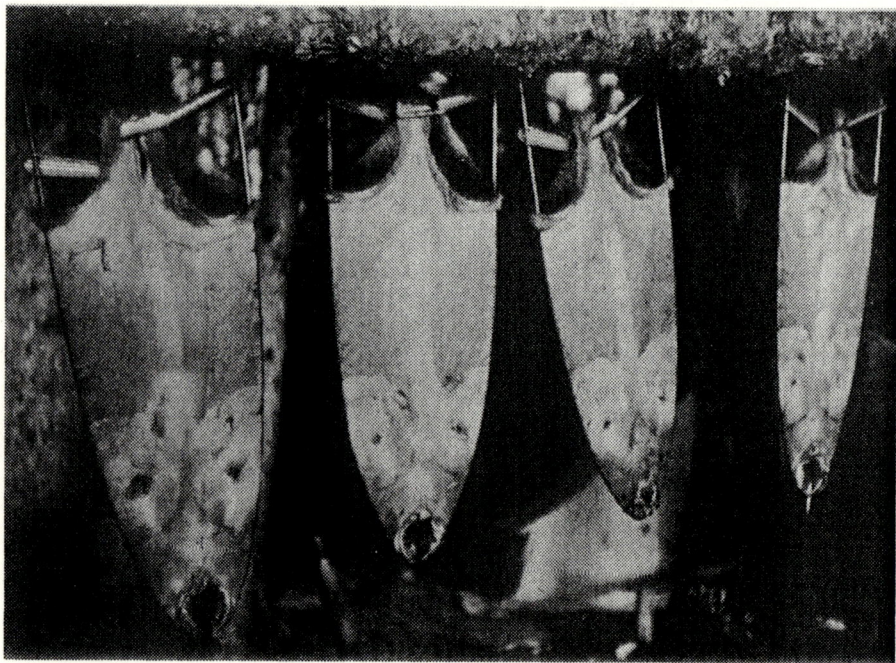

Muskrat pelts drying on stretchers, Fort Yukon, Alaska. (Photo by Richard A. Caulfield, Fairbanks, Alaska)

ing a paradox that could be called a "value inversion." In the two cultures that now stand face to face, the fur hunt culture and the antifur culture, diametrically opposed notions of luxury have become apparent. What is commonplace in the large urban centers— disposable cash income, an immense variety of goods behind each shop window, hot and cold running water, indoor toilet facilities, sophisticated and public transport, and so on—is luxury beyond all comprehension to the fur trapper in the Yukon Territory and the seal hunter from Ungava Bay. On the other hand, what is commonplace to them—lots of fresh air and clean, clear water, more than enough space for everyone on the land and on the water, plenty of unpolluted meat and fish, and beautiful warm skins and furs—is unattainable luxury to millions of people in Boston, Detroit, Rotterdam, and Berlin.

To answer the question, Is fur a luxury? one has to ask first, For whom? After all, luxury is a relative idea.

Of course, it is up to the individual to decide what is unacceptable luxury for him or for her. That is a subjective decision. But it is truly a strange experience for Athabascan Indians from the great forests of Alaska or for Inuit hunters from small settlements in Arctic Canada to be confronted with the idea that the only product that comes from their spartan daily lives, by the sweat of their brows, and the only thing from their world for which white people have ever had any use, now has become unacceptable because it is a luxury. And this is told to them by people who have refrigerators, freezers, cars in their garages, and two color television sets in their bungalows and take yearly vacations in Miami or Costa del Sol.

A good-quality fur coat will last half a lifetime. If you consider the wear and the value that you get for the money, this is not a luxury. It is a good investment. But people do not think of it this way. People think, it is a luxury to own so beautiful a piece of apparel even if it is not particularly expensive in relation to the quality. They can be embarrassed by wearing and showing off such luxury, because deep down there is still a little bit of the puritan in most of us.

The desire to dress up and embellish oneself is nothing to be ashamed of. It is in itself only a harmless extravagance of the kind that makes life a little less gray and tedious. Any claim that adornment is available only to the rich, a mark of indecent consumerism in the middle of a poor world, is an outright lie. The inhabitants of

Gwich'in Athabaskan elder Nathaniel Frank, of Venetie, Alaska, wearing caribou parka.
(Photo by Richard A. Caulfield, Fairbanks, Alaska)

the Stone Age designed ornaments and decorations on their tools. Some markings might very well have had a magical purpose, but others assuredly were only for decoration. Women, and increasing numbers of men, rich and poor, wear earrings just for the look of them. Who can blame them for that?

Broby Johansen, a Danish ethnographer who has written extensively about the history of clothing, comments about the Inuit women's dress of Greenland: "The women cut and sew their costumes, and decorate them with multi-colored geometrical patterns in an appliqué technique with small, sewn-on colored square skin pieces, skin ribbons pulled through holes in the skin, and embroidery done with hair from the caribou. These extravagant decorations, consisting of pin-sized dots of intense color sewn upon this very utilitarian costume, display the same *nonutilitarian poetry* as that shown in Eskimo verse."[4]

In our Judeo-Christian culture there has always been an element of self-righteous puritanism. Call it Manichaeism, Jansenism, puritanism, or what you will, the main element is the same thing: the human being's spontaneous need for enjoyment and self-expression, for exuberance and joy, for "nonutilitarian poetry," has always been stamped as sinful or at the very least indecent. We still have such bigots in our midst and probably will never completely rid ourselves of them: people who are outraged by a wrap of white fox or a sealskin coat with wolverine decorations simply because it is beautiful and luxurious, people for whom embellishment is "empty vanity." For them the nobility and the beauty of the product are reason enough to call it an indecency.

This attitude is simply not legitimate.

Morality and the Killing of Wild Animals

Compassion for animals is not a modern phenomenon. Hinduism, which is pervaded by the respect for everything living, has for thousands of years motivated humans to reflect on their relationship with animals. The Mosaic writings, which are between two and three thousand years old, are unequivocal in their view that animals have to be treated decently. Saint Francis of Assisi seems to have had an unusual ability to communicate with animals and birds; that he felt something special for them cannot be doubted. All these things have left their imprint on Western culture, which is otherwise characterized by its propensity for cruelty and death, sometimes hidden behind and sometimes plainly apparent within all its courteous behavior, its civilized articulateness, and its nationalistic and colonialistic rationalizations.

Maybe the current animal-protection furor is caused by increasing frustration over the unmitigated aggressiveness of humans in this shrinking world of ours, over all those who persecute, subjugate, torture, and kill each other, who produce endless stockpiles of atomic bombs, who poison nomads' wells in the desert and mob children in their schoolyards, who, to put it bluntly, are incorrigible. Maybe it is because of this frustration that so many are turning toward an area where at least something can be done. After all, the animals are completely innocent. Why should they be made to suffer?

In our problem-filled and contentious everyday life, we have at least one small breathing hole: television often shows very beautiful nature programs, some from exotic places around the world, some from the small areas of untouched nature still found here and there in the industrialized world. Here there is still something that functions as the Creator would have wanted it to function; here there is no evil or intrigue.

And then we hear that also here, exactly here, there are people who trap, harpoon, shoot, and kill. Is there no one to set a limit on such behavior? Why cannot the animals be left in peace?

It is no wonder that people who have grown up on concrete sidewalks and know nature only from television react in this way. It could hardly be otherwise. The question whether it is moral or immoral to kill, not just wild animals but any kind of animal, seems to be one that grows ever larger in this urban world, alienated as it is from nature. Without question there is an ethical dimension to the relationship between animals and humans. But how do we deal with this matter?

In genuine hunting cultures of the past, as well as in those still in existence, the ethical dimension is inherent in the respect that hunters show their prey. In 1741 the Danish Lutheran minister and missionary Hans Egede wrote about the Greenlanders: "When they go whale catching, they put on their best gear and apparel, as if they were going to a wedding feast, fancying that if they did not come cleanly and neatly dressed, the whale, who cannot bear slovenly and

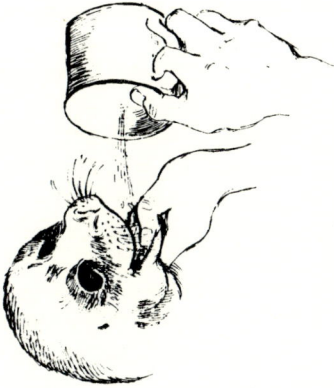

The old Greenlandic hunting traditions build on respect for the prey. For example, when a seal has been brought into the house, ancient rules dictate that water shall be poured into its mouth at once. Thus it will be made to feel how happy people are to have it, and more seals will follow. (Drawing by Jens Rosing in Finn Lynge, *Fugl og Sael og Menneskesjael*, Copenhagen, 1981)

dirty habits, would shun them and fly from them."[5] The old Greenlanders' traditions tell us that out of respect for their nature as birds, ptarmigans have to be brought into the house through the airing hole, in contrast to sea mammals, who should be brought in through the main entrance to avoid giving offense to them as creatures of the sea. Ptarmigan and caribou meat, similarly, should not be boiled together with seal or whale meat. Ravens' nests may not be plundered for eggs, because otherwise the ravens will take revenge by spoiling the hunt. And one should not show disrespect toward the fish by throwing fish bones in the urine pail, because then the fish will disappear. Seals, whales, birds, fish—everything living has the right to a minimum of respect.

The ethical dimension is important, and nobody can accuse traditional hunters of immorality. The killing of animals in hunting cultures is commonplace and natural, so completely open that children view and participate in it without growing up to be psychopathic killers on that account.

If it is immoral to kill animals, then it is certainly also indecent to eat meat. The fence is no better than the thief. But the majority of humans still eat meat, and life in the Arctic regions is impossible without animal proteins. Are the cold-weather regions peopled with indecent men and women? That charge is hard to take seriously. This book is based on the premise that it is good to live in the Arctic and that meat is good food, healthy food, and decent food.

Human beings eat anything, just as pigs do. That is a sobering thought, rather than a flattering one, but let us be realistic. Human beings have been given both the herbivore molars and the carnivore incisors. It cannot be unethical to live the way nature has equipped us to do. Nature is not immoral!

But is it not possible to butcher only tame animals and let wild animals be? Should nature not be allowed to find its own balance, there where wild animals live, without the interference of humans? Is it not wrong to hunt and kill those beautiful creatures in their natural state?

In response to this argument, it should be pointed out, first of all, that all the talk about "nature's balance" is something of a myth. Nature, if left to itself, actually functions in a constant state of imbalance, often with enormous deviations. An example is the caribou of the Arctic. In good years, when moss and lichen are thick and abundant, the population of caribou grows very quickly. As the size of the herd increases, the amount of available food diminishes, because moss and lichen grow very slowly. Finally there are too many animals for a very limited food source, and as these food reserves become depleted, the caribou grow famished. The animals begin to starve. They are weakened and finally die of hunger and cold by the thousands, with incredible suffering, and the size of the herd is reduced enormously. Mosses and lichens grow back over time, and everything begins anew. That is nature's cruel swing of the pendulum.

When humans start to get involved, two new options appear: either ruthless exploitation that can totally destroy the animal population or, on the other hand, rational wildlife management that can keep the population relatively constant, so that the huge oscillations in population caused by nature can be prevented or at least limited. With good hunting traditions and some common sense, hunters can, if they want to, establish without any great problems a reasonable balance between themselves and nature's living resources. This is why there are very few examples of any contemporary hunting people's pushing a species to extinction, whereas the habitat destruction that follows industrial growth and general modern greed has been responsible for the extinction of thousands of species.

The large population of harp seals near Newfoundland has over time gone through most of the sequence that has just been described:

—an original population of unknown millions of animals untouched by humans that functioned in their own imbalance with the environment;

—a modest decimation by the local fishermen who settled the area, who used both the skin and the meat of the seal to the fullest, from adult seals as well as pups;

—a large-scale utilization during the 150 years from the end of the eighteenth century to the 1930s, the objective of which was the seal blubber—a harvest of the abundance of nature that left behind it a sustainable population;

—an intensification of the completely industrialized utilization of animals, where the interest moved from the blubber to the coat of the pups;

—a short period of ruthless exploitation caused by an uncoordinated and irrational industrial utilization;

—another quite short period, which saw intensive marine biological, veterinary, and police control over both the small fishermen's coast-based traditional seal pup hunt and the Norwegian-Canadian ship-based industrial hunt—control that once again brought the population to a stable period of growth;

—and finally, in reaction against the ruthless exploitation of the 1960s, a violent reduction of the hunt (the seal pup hunt has ceased, but there is still a certain harvest of adult animals), which in actual practice meant a complete freeing of the population, with its attendant uncontrolled growth. We still do not know the final effects of this growth on the ecological (im)balance. The wisdom of the present situation—no wildlife management at all—can readily be challenged.

No, it is not in itself immoral to kill wild animals. As a means of food procurement, it is a necessity for millions of people the world over, and it is imperative where people's living space and needs come into conflict with those of the animals.

There exists a species of wild animals whose interests in living and reproducing are at odds with the city dweller's way of life. Unlike other animals, these are exposed to full-scale chemical warfare in a businesslike and no-nonsense manner. Millions of these animals are allowed to die a slow, torturous death by poison. They are intelligent and capable of feeling pain, but they are ugly and repulsive. They have, urbanites conclude, no right to be there. They are rats.

Morality and the Killing of Newborn Animals

It is not by itself immoral to kill animals. It can sometimes be the only right thing. If a cat has too many kittens, as happens all the time, it is best to kill them instantly, preferably before there is any bonding between the kittens and their mother. It is an old tradition to drown such small kittens, but the most humane thing is actually to cut their heads off. One thing is sure: we should not wait till they become adults and get the well-known nine lives. Then there will be problems.

The same thing holds true for sheep babies, cow babies, and chicken babies—commonly called lambs, calves, and chicken. There is a long tradition of killing them, and eating them. The protest against the "immoral" animal baby murders near Newfoundland has not given rise to similar waves of protest against the butchery traditions at home, nor has it given rise to boycotts of lambskin coats or chicken salads.

The difference—people will say—is that near Newfoundland the pups were butchered while they were still suckling their mothers; they were killed right in front of their mothers, where it was most painful! But that claim is not true. The harp seals' suckling period is very short, about ten days. The baby is born with a yellow fur that changes to the famous whitecoat three days or so after its birth. After a week to two weeks as a whitecoat the baby seal stops suckling its mother, who now leaves its baby and is no longer interested in it. The mother animal jumps into the water next to the ice floe and immediately gets caught up in a new mating game. It is only when these ten days had passed that the hunters showed up.

Of course, with the large number of animals involved, there were some variations in the pattern, and certainly hunters came across pups whose mothers had not yet left them. In these cases the hunters did not touch the animals, if for no other reason than that they were in a hurry.

What then is moral and immoral in the killing of newborns? Public opinion does not seem to condemn the practice in near and known contexts, but people become very upset when it takes place in an unfamiliar context. It is difficult to take that kind of thinking very seriously.

Both farmers and hunters agree not to interfere in the symbiotic relationship between the mother animal and her pup during suckling. If the young ones are to be killed, it has to be immediately after birth and before suckling starts or soon after the suckling period is finished. Nothing here is especially immoral.

Organizational Success and Cultural Confrontations

There is not much rationality in the battle that was waged against the seal hunt near Newfoundland. In reality, the objections to the harvest were so insubstantial that it is hard to understand how the antisealing campaigns managed to gain such strength. Nevertheless, the fact is that it was the greatest animal-protection case in the world to date.

The reason for its success lay first and foremost in the brilliant idea that somebody got to call this specific animal pup a *baby*. It is true that the whitecoat pup is unusually appealing: it has wonderful snow-white fur and big black eyes; it is helpless, awkward in a cute way, and extremely photogenic. Without question, an image like this was a gift to any advertising agent. If opponents of the hunt showed images of some huge, ugly man who came to club these incredibly cute baby animals with a baseball bat so that their brains were strewn all over the snow and ice, then, yes, no doubt, many people would spill their coffee all over their tables as they cried out, "This is baby murder!"

At this point, no rational interpretations would help. Nobody wanted to listen to explanations about wildlife management, or the seasonal income of poor people, or the interest of the fishing industry. All such comment fell on deaf ears. The only thing that mattered was that this awful butchery had to stop!

Countless children in the world go hungry, are forced into prostitution in Bangkok, are penned up in cruel state institutions in Romania, roam the streets of Harlem, or die in senseless wars. These desperate children rouse our attention through the media. In orderly societies like ours, countless others are beaten by their parents behind closed doors or go loveless through an uncaring world. Honestly, aren't most of us overwhelmed by helplessness, to the point where our feelings approach callousness, when faced with these horrors? However, when it came to the baby seals, we were facing something that could be remedied. Do we have subconscious or unconscious fear or guilt over the fate of the children of the world, psychological suppressions that are compensated for through reactions toward these baby animals?[6] This is a question a clinical psychologist might have something to say about. The rest of us can only notice that here somehow a button is pressed that activates a primeval force in people's reactions. Here is something that nothing rational can match. Anyone who in a convincing manner can paint a picture of his or her opponent as a child murderer has won the day.

When this charge first began to surface, it became abundantly clear that the anti-seal-hunt campaign would draw everyone who could crawl or walk from all the animal-protection societies. Their reaction was not really surprising. It is an honest matter to engage oneself in animal protection, just as it is honest—though not terribly smart—to be of the opinion that these hunters could just stop their way of life and start growing potatoes instead.

What was much more surprising was that the organizations that traditionally dealt with ecology jumped on the bandwagon and remained committed to the antisealing movement even after it had stopped being an ecological concern. At least since the early 1970s, no responsible group of scientists could be made to say anything but that the population of harp seals near Newfoundland was doing well. With the hunt quotas Canada and Norway had agreed on, with the veterinary and police control that kept the regulations observed, and with the constant scientific supervision and analysis of the population that the various marine biological teams carried out, the population was secure. As a matter of fact, it had entered a period of stable growth. There had indeed been a threat to the population in the mid-1950s, as noted earlier, but that threat had now been removed. At this point one might have expected that, for example, Greenpeace would leave the matter alone and let the animal-protection agencies deal with it, because Greenpeace is an ecological movement.

But no, Greenpeace stayed out on the ice floes and sprayed the seals with paint, year after year, and Greenpeace was the main actor on the European scene, together with IFAW, when the European Community's seal pup directive was debated.

Why?

The demarcation line between the ecological and animal welfare movements was blurred during these years. Emphasis shifted in two directions at the same time. Some of the ecological movements (though not all of them) began to incorporate also an animal-protection posture, and the animal-protection organizations began spouting an ecological rhetoric. The result was, predictably enough, a growing confusion among the public about what the word *ecological* really means. Contrary to what the ordinary animal-protection organizations want to do, the ecological organizations' concerns are much more with the health of nature's processes. An animal population's and, of course, an animal species' survival and well-being are ecological concerns, but not what happens to the individual animals. In many situations the ecological concerns are closely related to wildlife management. True ecologists are not necessarily opposed to hunting.

But now these useful and clear distinctions became hazy, and to this day they remain confused to the general public. If you ask people, you are quite often told that ecology has to do with something called environmental consciousness. That is the catch word of the moment. If you are environmentally conscious, you cannot accept the killing of animal pups in Canada. That's how simple it is—to some.

To others, of course, this development represents a challenge. The Canadian Arctic Resources Committee (CARC), for example, a nongovernment, nonprofit organization known for its long-standing and eminent work in matters of Arctic ecology, is adamant that the demarcation line between animal welfare and ecological concerns must remain clear. The same thing goes—in principle at least—for the World Wide Fund for Nature (WWF), as well as for many less well known conservation-oriented groups and organizations. Many people are well aware that clear thinking in this matter is a favor done to all parties.

Another factor is the money implicated. In 1981 the East Canadian seal hunt brought in $13 million. Of this, just over half went to the approximately two thousand Inuit who lived off the hunt, taking adult seals, and the three thousand or so fishermen in Newfoundland who had the seal pup hunt as an extra job. Traditionally a Newfoundlander earned about $2,000 from the hunt every year, and an Inuit hunter approximately $450.

After the antisealskin directive issued by the European Economic Community (EEC) in 1983 had started to have its effect, the total national income from the hunt fell from $13 million to under $3 million. The seal hunters' income fell from $7 million to $1.3 million.

The individual Newfoundland fisherman's income from this hunt fell from $2,000 to under $400 a year. The Inuit's income fell to an all-time low of about $100. However, the anti-seal-hunt organizations were strengthened financially to a remarkable degree.[7] In the middle of the 1980s, IFAW made more than $6 million on its seal-hunt campaign. In the United States alone, the seal pups reaped $5 million for Greenpeace. Defenders of Wildlife (USA) got over $1.7 million in 1981 and the Center for Environmental Education (also USA), which specialized in the anti-seal-hunt campaign, made $2.2 million in 1980. In Germany it was the seal campaign that was instrumental in establishing Greenpeace as a major organization and that managed to put its budget in the black. The German biologist Wolfgang Fischer said on German television in January 1990: "It was important at that time that Greenpeace become a big organization. Greenpeace was very small and I thought that it was quite legitimate to use a cute animal with big eyes."[8] Fischer was the campaign manager for Greenpeace in Germany from 1982, and he knew what he was talking about. Today Greenpeace-Germany has an annual income of DM 50 million.

Once organizations have grown big, they *get* huge amounts of money and *use* huge amounts of money. Constant spending is the criterion that keeps everything moving. Greenpeace operates with ships, rubber rafts, and helicopters. That costs a lot of money. In 1982 IFAW used $1 million in half a year just for newsletters and postage. The organization furthermore used a million dollars for a house with offices and computer equipment, as well as a car, a helicopter, and an airplane. In 1984 IFAW threatened to get involved in a Canadian parliamentary election by means of a $3 million political campaign aimed at candidates that supported the seal hunt.

At least seven environmental groups offer their presidents a yearly salary of more than $100,000, but competition in the field is tough. Most of the well-known organizations pay their leaders somewhere between $30,000 and $85,000 a year, far from the largest salaries, but still impressive from the vantage point of the Arctic hunters.[9]

Nothing in this world is simple and clear-cut. It remains true that a great many people do a lot of hard environmentally oriented work at a fraction of the salaries they could obtain in private business, if they so chose. Much practical idealism is at work here, maybe especially in the many smaller and less well known grass-roots environmentalist groups. Yet on the whole, from the Arctic indigenous peoples' perspective, environmentalism has become an establishment, with concomitant finances. Money comes, money goes—big money.

The awful thing about it, as we all know, is that initially a few people will build an empire and determine the course of the capital flow. Later on, it is the flow of money that decides the course of the people involved.

The seal pup hunt off Newfoundland *has* been stopped. The battle *has* been won. The Newfoundland fishermen *have* been defeated; the Inuit hunting economy *has* been destroyed, their livelihood criminalized. The outcome of this struggle was certainly neither proper or reasonable, yet it was termed a political necessity. The job of the seal hunter has now been relegated to the lowest place in society, a despicable profession nobody wants to advertise, a hate object of the entire world.

One would think that this would be enough. But no: the organizations are there; they have their ships and helicopters and computers and public relations systems; the jobs of many people depend on it all functioning; money must flow. So on we go! Now the focus shifts—bite by bite, slice by slice—to the whalers, the few who are left, and the trappers of the great forests, among them the Indians of Alaska and Canada.

In the 1960s and 1970s, when the public's attention started to focus on the seal pup hunt near Newfoundland, the general consensus among the Inuit of Canada and Greenland was that it didn't concern them. The controversy was in Newfoundland, and was centered on a traditional hunt of seal pups as well as on an industrial hunt of both pups and adults. Both are non-Inuit styles of hunt. It was not their war!

That opinion has been corrected. As the campaigns moved forward, the price of sealskins fell and fell, not only of whitecoats but of all seal skins. The hunters in the small Inuit settlements of the Canadian Arctic and of Greenland slowly but surely were reduced to what they had never thought they should become, receivers of social welfare. A complete culture started to falter. Gradually, it dawned on the northerners that the seal hunters among them, the traditionally completely self-reliant part of the population, no longer had an econ-

One of the 1989 products from the Greenland Tannery was called "Bardot" and was made from ringed seal. In Denmark, it has once more become fashionable to don a sealskin coat, though this is not yet so elsewhere in Europe, to say nothing of the United States. (Great Greenland Inc., Glostrup, Denmark)

omy of any consequence to fall back upon. They had become sacrificial lambs for the benefit of some warriors who were completely unconcerned about whether or not a few Eskimos got hurt.

The effects of the repeated antisealskin campaigns and the European Council's antisealskin directive[10] have been documented many times. It is true that both the Greenlanders and the Canadian Inuit are exempt from the directive, but this exemption has not resulted in any discernible differences. Sealskin has become virtually impossible to sell.[11]

Maybe the policy will change again in the coming years. Fortunately, there is something that seems to indicate a change of attitude, at least for the moment, in Denmark. Many people know that what had happened has been extremely unfair to the Greenlandic hunters and the Inuit in Canada. Many in the WWF, as well as within the United Nations Environment Programme (UNEP), the scientific research organizations, and the national governments with a responsible attitude toward their aboriginal peoples and their way of life, are now starting to understand the real connections and consequences. They have become ready to make an effort to stop the emotional nonsense that has flourished in the hothouses of misinformation. And let it also be remembered that Greenpeace has come with an official apology to the Greenlandic seal hunters for all the unintentional damage its campaign has caused the Inuit.[12]

These are positive elements in a serious and difficult situation. But they change nothing in the overall picture. This is not an ordinary debate between alternative opinions. It is a struggle between cultures, wherein one—earnestly and with a great deal of self-righteousness—believes itself to have a natural authority to dictate how things ought to be.

And that of course means war.

3 ◆ The Whale War

Just as the whale has always been the mightiest and most magnificent of all catches for the hunters of the polar sea, it has now become the strongest of all symbols in the world of nature, which any schoolchild anywhere knows is threatened. The symbolic function of the whale has been so strong that it has become a myth. Only a very, very small fraction of the thousands of people who support the campaign against whale hunting have ever seen a whale. For them the whale is a silhouette on the horizon, the knowledge of something big, beautiful, and mysterious deserving to live. For them it seems to be the whale in the singular that is threatened. These people have no idea that only certain species are endangered, whereas other species have never come close to being threatened. Neither do most have any idea that there are many people around the world who are nutritionally dependent on a whale hunt that does not threaten the existence of the animals.

Information of this kind is unpopular. It is twisted, repressed, or silenced. The myth must not be threatened.

Myth and Behavior

As a result of general egocentricity, the conservationist nations believe that they are the only ones with any sympathy for whales. This is not the case. Whales are a myth all over the world, in whaling societies as well as in those societies that have never lifted a weapon against these magnificent animals.

In the old Eskimo myths whales have overwhelming significance. These incredible animals are not only food, a mountain of meat,

Humpback whale, southeast Alaska (Photo by Richard A. Caulfield, Fairbanks, Alaska)

blubber, and muktuk, they are also a challenge to the best in the hunter. The whale, they believe, wants to be hunted only by a hunter in clean clothes. It is a clean animal itself and will not put up with anything less. Should anyone sin by using a deceased hunter's cast-off harpoon against it, the whale will evade capture. On the other hand, it readily allows itself to be taken with newly fashioned, well-crafted hunting gear. It knows the taboos. That there has to be order in things and respect for the animals' feelings has been the Arctic hunter's basic world order since ancient times.[1]

Despite its narrowness and all its limitations, the old Inuit world was amazingly great. It was a world where a man gave his daughter away in marriage to a blue fox, where a whale fell in love with a young maiden from the village. This is the universe where the soul of the bard wandered through creation from grass straw to polar bear, expanding the spiritual horizons of the audience so that they could experience everything living from within. By an apparent paradox, these hunting people, who can survive only as refined experts in killing, possess the deepest respect for their prey.

When Knud Rasmussen reached Alaska on his great dogsled journey in 1926, he was told—at the hearth of the whole Thule cul-

Sea mammals, womanhood, and creation merge in the ancient Inuit myth known as "Mother of the Seas." She inhabits the ocean depths and controls all things living (and edible) there. In times of famine and bad hunting luck, the shamans would go into a trance and travel to the Mother's abode. There, they would attempt to appease her anger over all the broken taboos, prevailing on her to release all the good animals that were destined for the Inuit. (Keld Hansen, *Tanker og Streger*, Skjern, Denmark, 1991. Drawing by the author)

ture's strong whaling tradition—the myth known as "The Whale's Soul and Its Burning Heart." The whale's heart and soul is here a young and gracious woman, hospitable but restless and uneasy, who in return for her friendliness demands only that one taboo be respected: no one may touch the wick in the little train oil lamp that lights up the house, which is really the inside of the whale. This flame is its heart. But the visiting raven man, stupid and curious as he is, cannot resist: he touches the sacred wick. The girl dies and the whale turns into a carcass. And the raven man, who "out of pure curiosity . . . had touched a heart and destroyed something noble and beautiful, . . . bragged loudly: I killed the whale! I killed the whale! It was me who killed it! —And he became a great man among the people."[2]

There are many major elements in this strange myth. There is the sexual—the raven is a male who penetrates the female whale. The whole idea of the inside of the whale's "house" has a clear sexual undertone, a familiar aspect of the sagas and myths of the Inuit. The element of rape points in the same direction. The raven does not have sensitivity enough for the young maiden's inner fire; he is selfish and takes exactly what she so pointedly asks him to leave alone—and she is burned out.

The raven is an insignificant person, for he has no respect for the taboo. The life and behavior of the Eskimos of old were regulated by taboos that had to be observed, whatever the cost. Those who did not know their place and obey the rules would find themselves punished by life, with accidents, failed hunts, famine, or, as here, by having the quality of life diminished—because that is what happens in this myth: revenge does not take the form of either hunger or misfortune; it comes as a moral degeneracy that affects the entire small society. People are blinded by the repulsive little braggart who not only sets himself above the rules of decency but even boasts about it. The disaster for the inconsiderate hunter is that he loses his dignity. Thus, in the end, there is a parallel between the hunt and sexuality. In both cases, it is necessary to nurture a measure of respect and mutual consideration for the prize, which is the partner. Sinning against the fundamental demand for respect for the woman or for the prey is an insult to life itself: her breath dies out, and the living flesh turns into a carcass.

Inversely, when the hunter respects the ancient rules and taboos, he is led to an attachment and reverence for the prey that can best be likened to the sentiments a man feels for his beloved. Just as, in a human relationship, love can wither, so can the hunter become insensitive to the animals upon which he feeds; his feelings can die

Whaling demands undivided attention from the hunters. In addition, the whale tolerates no activity on land for the duration of the hunt. If these rules are not respected, the whale will take revenge. (Drawing by Jens Rosing in Finn Lynge, *Fugl og Sael og Menneskesjael*, Copenhagen, 1981)

away, and with them, alas, his own self-esteem as well. But love between man and woman can also thrive, and among the true leaders
of the small hunting community one can always find those whose
ways and sentiments are dictated by respect for the prey and the rules
of the hunt. Those hunters' families will never go hungry: the animals will seek them out, as if asking to be taken.

Feelings?

In November 1988 a lecture was given at the Zoology Museum in
Copenhagen, followed by a discussion, on Danish attitudes in the
International Whaling Commission (IWC). One member of the audience presented the point of view that considering the official policies of the scientists' home countries, the scientific results of the commission's work seemed to be predictable. And since, in other words,
the scientific reports were considered by some to be largely a costume put on over preexisting attitudes, then would it not be simpler
just to present the basic emotional standpoints?

This question was not meant arrogantly. It was meant as a reasonable proposal, worth serious consideration—which it is.

It is true enough that scientists in the IWC are divided into two
camps concerning the question of scientific studies of whaling. One
of the issues in the debate is whether it is a good idea to kill whales
in order to increase the existing fund of knowledge about their ages,
sex, what they eat, and so on. Some say yes, others no. Those saying
yes come from whaling nations like Iceland, Norway, and Japan,
which are first in line to reopen commercial whaling if possible when
the moratorium runs out. Those saying no are scientists from the
countries that have abandoned all whaling, or that have never had
any commercial interests in it. It is well known that these countries
have ridden the wave of antiwhaling feelings for years.

The political position on whaling will necessarily reflect a division
of this nature. But what about the evaluations of scientists? Don't
many of us carry around the idea that science is objective, something
not dictated by politics?

In the 1960s a number of minor sea battles, called the Cod War,
were fought in the waters around Iceland. The Icelanders claimed
their rights first to a fifty-mile, and later to a two hundred-mile,
fishing boundary. English trawlers were shoved outside the two

hundred-mile limit, and the process was often rough. The many and dramatic collisions at sea filled the front pages of the newspapers and naturally led to voluble political rhetoric, intense diplomatic activity, and—last but not least—an intensification of the marine biological research concerning the fish population around Iceland. Most of this research was carried out by the International Council for the Exploration of the Sea (ICES), which has its headquarters in Copenhagen.

It is interesting that the ICES's research during the Cod War was not accused of political bias. Research was research; estimates of the fish population's size were based on biological factors. Fishing policies, which were frankly political, were a separate matter. In the ICES English and Icelandic marine biologists worked side by side with all the others involved. How the politicians wanted to use the results of their work was seen as an unrelated decision.[3]

But on the unremittingly problematic question of the relation between advisory science and political, decision-making processes, the ICES and the IWC differ in a marked way. An organization can decide to try to keep science and politics separated or to work scientifically from politically chosen premises. Both approaches are, in their own ways, respectable enough, so long as no attempt is made to disguise the character of the work accomplished. An attempt of that sort is, of course, never respectable.

Now a knowledgeable reader may object that this portrayal is oversimplified. Differences between the two organizations are not as clear-cut as all that, it may be said. There are scientists in the IWC who sincerely try to maintain a cool and objective distance from the often heated debate concerning whaling, people who want to reach the most objective data possible; and looking at it from the other side, it is certainly possible to find in the work done at the ICES over the years examples of scientific advice that comes suspiciously close to the respective advisers' national fishing policies.[4]

Well, that is possible. You can always find exceptions to the rule, and the difference between the two forums is not absolute. But the work done in the IWC has developed a different profile from that of the ICES. It is reasonable to question the IWC's work as too politically charged. Perhaps the various national delegations at the IWC's meetings should be encouraged to base their recommendations on philosophical and emotional grounds, without trying to cloak them in statistics or other scientific garb. It is honest to have feelings. Why not try to express them, or even discuss them? Then we would all get closer to the heart of the matter.

Warm and Cold

Why is there such a disparity between the ICES and the IWC? One fact is certain: the ICES concerns itself with fish, whereas the IWC regulates the hunting and killing of mammals. This in itself makes a difference, and it is apparently a crucial distinction in terms of deep psychology. Quite simply, we feel something for warm-blooded animals that we don't feel for cold-blooded ones. Only a few people will ever let themselves become emotionally upset over a mullet. On the other hand, most feel something special about a beautiful and graceful furbearing animal. There is undeniably a difference between a cold, silent fish and a warm, alert animal. What is a whale in this connection? Naturally, it is something in between. For a long time, the whale was considered a kind of fish, and as long as this was the case, the public did not react much more dramatically about the "whale fisheries" than people have always done—and do—about fishing in general. But as people became more informed, they realized that the whale is a mammal, warm-blooded and in many ways fascinating, and in turn their emotional response has changed. Of course, this reaction is felt in the Whaling Commission, which is besieged by animal-protection and environmental organizations as the ICES has never been.

There certainly is a difference between the people concerning themselves with fish and those who deal with sea mammals. Biologists are people, too, and their emotional reactions are part of a conscious or unconscious interplay with their intellects.

There is something magnetic, obsessive—something that seems to be pure magic—about whales. They are mammals that live in water. Psychologists tell us that water represents some of the deepest and most fundamental emotions in the human mind. In interpreting dreams, the occurrence of rain or floods or streams is considered particularly interesting. Experiences presented in such a framework are among the strongest and most significant, embedded in the deepest layer of our subconscious, where they act with a strength we do not really appreciate. They mobilize what psychologists call "the oceanic feeling," a dimension that, according to some authors, comes from a fundamental, unconscious memory of what life was like in the mother's womb.[5]

For whatever reason, we are faced with strong stuff when we talk about whales. Emotional reactions come out that cannot be disregarded. The public does react differently depending on whether the animal under consideration is a marine mammal or a four-footed land animal. You don't see Greenpeace joining the humane societies' campaigns against the trapping of furbearing animals.[6] But Greenpeace was on the baby-seal bandwagon in Newfoundland long after the genuine ecological concerns related to this case had been resolved. From the beach and outward, the oceanic feeling rules.

Money

A symbol that in only a few decades has managed to attain a mythical function is potent stuff.

First, it is obvious that when people let themselves be mobilized against whaling it is because they rebel against the plundering of nature's resources, an exploitation that presses against the very limits of life. People find it unbearable to continue learning about new species of animals that are threatened with extinction. Someone, they decide, must do something about it! This is a motive that has grown stronger and stronger. UNEP, the World Conservation Union (IUCN), the WWF, the Brundtland Commission, and all the environmental ministries of the world are pushing in the same direction. And with good reason: overexploitation of the world's resources is the basic threat hanging over all our heads.

Second, behind the above-board motive lies another and more complicated one: industrialized society's moral scruples about the motives by which it is itself controlled, that is, money and profit. There are different kinds of whaling, but *commercial* whaling is the kind that is conceived of as dirty and unbearable. That people kill whales to eat them can be accepted, as incomprehensible as it might seem. But killing a whale to make money is at the bottom of the pit! Indignation gets mobilized here, which is fed by more than the feelings people have for a species considered to be threatened. This indignation builds on people's continually repressed reaction against the commercial motive of profit per se. From a Jungian perspective, the profit society seems to have created a safety valve here, through which the excessive pressure from the dark side of society can be let out.[7] All of society's basic mechanisms are connected to monetary profit; everybody knows that, and everyone accepted it ages ago. Still, a worm eats at the heart; there is a little voice that won't be quiet and that keeps on whispering: this can't be right, all this competition about money is degrading, there must be higher values in life! When environmental organizations call out the troops for battle against commercial whaling, they give this little voice an unexpectedly loud and impressive resonance, and it turns into a shout: No! Not money and profit at the expense of this wonder of nature!

There is a shrillness in the voice, a certain bitterness in the rhetoric of the antiwhaling campaigners that—unwittingly—signals what they really feel about their own society's primary motivation and basic value, *money*: when the race for money materializes as a hunt on the strongest symbol of nature in our time, they say no. Money must not destroy nature. But this is exactly what money does when it creates a profit-maximizing mechanism that eats away at resources until they are used up. That is what money has always done in an industrialized world.

Must money always work this way?

Maximizing Profits and the Subsistence Life-style

In Europe in the Middle Ages, it was not considered in good taste to demand interest on debts. It was considered usury and therefore a sin. This attitude has been modified since then, as we all know, and now only the charging of unreasonably high interest rates is called usury. A reasonable interest rate not only is considered acceptable but has become a kind of accumulator in the economic system. How would growth be organized if the banks didn't charge interest? How would banks exist at all?

Maximizing profits is simply our world's motivation. That is what modern life is all about. For hundreds of thousands of years, people have tried to get enough to live from hand to mouth, with a few stores set aside for the winter. But in our day people are concerned with making their possessions breed and breed again, so that they become rich—become millionaires, billionaires! The dream, which is reality for quite a few, is of having far, far more than they can possibly eat, drink, or enjoy in any way. The goal is the impressive columns in their accounts. We all know that these impressive numbers have at some time cost some other people a considerable amount of sweat and work that has been poorly paid. The accumulated figures have presumably cost the oppression of others, and a lot of social injustice along the way. That's just the way things are. The world is not perfect. The possibility that the entire system is sick is not one we enjoy thinking about.

Many people have discovered that the system *is* sick, not because the process of maximizing profits treads on fellow human beings along the way—this leaves us cold—but because it is becoming more and more obvious that nature's resources cannot last indefinitely. The lust for profit eats away at the rainforests of the Amazon, destroys life in the oceans with drift nets, and drives the rhinoceros mercilessly into extinction. Had the IWC not in the late 1960s adopted the protective measures needed, the blue whale would have been a mere saga today.

But the blue whale was saved at the last minute. And then came the battle over commercial whaling as such, the stirring of world opinion and the forcing through of a moratorium.[8] It was an impressive feat. No wonder the continued work of the IWC has the special attention of environmental organizations. Their point now is to see to it that no commercial whaling ever starts up again, because money means profit and there are certain types of resources that simply cannot survive the profit-maximizing process. They get used up.

The logic is simple: the minute money enters an enterprise there is a take-over of power. Money takes control of people. Even though no one wants the resource—in this case whales—to become extinct, it happens anyway. The irresistible mechanism in this take-over is maximizing profits. No one can resist it and it runs out its line, all the way out.

This is why environmental organizations are such eager guardians in their lobbying to make sure that the only recurrent form of acceptable whale hunt, aboriginal subsistence whaling, is not contaminated by money.[9] If the particular species and populations are not threatened, they reason, it is all right for Greenlanders and Eskimos in Alaska to take a reasonable number of whales for local consumption—provided that there is no money in the hunt, because once money enters the scene, commercialization becomes unavoidable and the resource will be threatened. Or so it is claimed.

This is the hub of the conflict, and the battle will stand at this point for years to come. For this claim is not an accurate one. Money does not *necessarily* have to play a profit-maximizing role.

If we look back to the West Greenland of the old days—the whalers' Eldorado for centuries—we see a clear pattern.[10] From the 1600s and far into the nineteenth century, the large whaling fleets came to this area, attracted primarily by bowhead blubber and baleen. Before the great era of whaling the bowhead was to be found in large numbers all over the North Atlantic, but probably in highest concentration around Spitzberg, toward Jan Mayen and the northern part of the Denmark Strait, and in the Davis Strait. The commercial hunt followed the aforementioned order. First the European commercial whalers pillaged the waters around Spitzberg, and when that region was no longer profitable, they moved their activities farther away, to the west. The last area of permanent, massive activity was the west coast of Greenland, where, from their kayaks and sod huts on the beaches, the Greenlanders witnessed the systematic and effective thinning out of the prey their forefathers had hunted as they migrated from the north coast of Alaska toward the east and north of what is now Arctic Canada. The bowhead was the perfect prey for the Inuit whale hunters in their small skin boats. It is a slow swimmer and, in contrast to certain other species, not an especially intelligent animal. It is relatively easy both to encircle and to catch. Killing such a giant, though always dangerous, is nonetheless possible, and it provides large amounts of food and vitamins.

The Europeans went about things in a different manner. They brought mother ships with fast rowing dories they could set into the water when the whale was sighted. They performed their jobs with steel-tipped harpoons and steel spears and flensing blades—a material and quality unknown in the Inuit tradition. They were determined and effective. Because their concern was money and profit, they took only blubber and baleen; the rest was thrown away. The blubber was melted to train oil, which was sold to the light companies at home in London, Amsterdam, and Copenhagen. The baleen was made into combs and supports for crinolines and corsets.

The outcome was inevitable. The whaling captains were not given orders to ensure that the stocks remained able to survive this form of exploitation. It was the viability not of the whale population but of the economy that counted. The ships had to be depreciated, the crew had to be paid, the company had to make a profit. The attitude was, "What I don't take, someone else will. Just go to it!" And they did.

When, sometime in the nineteenth century, the party ended, and the last Englishman had sailed home, the bowhead whales off West Greenland had been all but exterminated. Of course, there were a number of other large species of whales left—blue, fin, sperm, minke, and sei whales, and some humpbacks—but of all these, only the latter was a slow enough swimmer to be suitable as prey for the traditional hunters. The Inuit who had served on board the Dutch and English ships had learned how to conduct a collective hunt with fast wooden rowing boats, however. And so, up to the late 1920s, such hunts were organized by the native Greenlanders in the Danish colonies of West Greenland.[11]

But the Inuit were no longer a whaling people as they had been in the old days. The backbone of the tradition had been broken. Besides, the economy was undergoing a slow but sure restructuring. Money had made its way to Greenland, and with money in the system, was not the essence of the old hunting culture threatened with extinction?

This question has been the basis for many discussions, even controversies. For my own part, I say no. The hunt culture, or as they call it in the IWC, the *subsistence life-style*, the ability to live directly off the resources of wild nature, is still in existence, though now with money involved. For money plays a different role for the Greenland hunters than it did for the Dutch and English whalers.

The role of money in the modern hunter society has nothing to do with depreciation of investments or payment of crews. As far as such things are necessary, they are financed with the money that circulates through the fisheries. Seals and whales are hunted for their meat, and the meat that is taken is distributed to everyone on land who is interested. The distribution is performed along guidelines based partly on the old rules about *hunt shares* and partly on the fact that many people who are not covered by these traditional regulations do want to have some of the meat and do have money. Money is needed by all the hunters to buy many daily commodities. Money is the only means of exchange that can open the channels of distribution in a modern society. The fact is that everybody wants meat, but only a small part of the population lives in places where landing this meat is the general way of life. There, far more meat is taken

One-fifth of Greenland's population subsists on sea mammals, and the hunters land far more meat than they can possibly eat. The scene is from Nuuk, Greenland, in the mid-1960s. (National Museum and Archives of Greenland)

than the local population can possibly eat. Therefore it is sold—for money.

Note, however, that the exchange of meat for money is not profit maximizing. Marine mammal hunting takes place either where no other livelihood is possible, in the traditional hunting communities where profit is an unknown concept, or as a by-product for people who write off their investments and earn their profits in fishing, not in whaling. The life of a hunter has changed in many ways since the old days; anything else would be surprising. But the subsistence life-style has survived and functions now as an integral part of a modern and partially industrialized society—without endangering its soul. Seals and whales are caught and landed to be eaten and sold to who-ever wants the meat, but not with the aim of earning money. When that happens anyway, it is a welcome additional prize. It does not result in an increased pressure on the whale resources, as was the case with the large whaling fleets. It is simply a different economic situation.[12]

The Small Cetaceans

The controversy surrounding whaling is big, and it continues to grow. The agenda is not any longer just the large whales. Now the battle is also reaching the small cetaceans: dolphins, porpoises, pilot whales, belugas, narwhals, and so on. Everything suggests that this is about to become an Arctic politician's nightmare, a complicated emotional problem that refuses to go away, whatever is done with it, and with no solutions in sight.

Everyone who works with this problem can confirm that at present there is a hitherto-unknown polarization of opinions and attitudes toward sea mammals. Already by 1972 the United States had succeeded in passing the Marine Mammal Protection Act, under which no seal or whale hunting is allowed, sea lions and sea otters are completely protected, and all importation of products from sea mammals is strictly forbidden. Of course, there are exceptions. The Aleut people of the Pribilof Islands are still allowed to take a couple of thousand fur seals every year, the Alaska Inupiaq are still allowed a quota on the large bowhead whale near the Arctic Ocean (at the moment, 41 whales per year), and the industrial fishermen in the Pacific Ocean still have official permission to kill 20,500 dolphins every year in connection with their net fishing of tuna. But the tendency is clear, and these exceptions are being closely monitored. Whale killing is not popular.

Environmental movements around the world look to the United States as the flagship that sets the course. Attitudes and campaigns originating in the United States direct opinions among like-minded people everywhere else. It is therefore of interest for all of us that the long-term U.S. goal seems to be total protection of the world's oceans, except for the fisheries. There are even those who maintain that the future belongs to aquaculture: the growth and harvest in specific limited coastal zones of those fish species that are preferred on the dinner table, coupled with complete protection of the wild species living in the oceans.

If it gets this far some day, then the oldest cultural battle of the world will be finished. Agriculture will have won over the hunting culture, and the entire world will be divided into three parts: settlement areas; areas at sea and on land that are tilled and cared for and from which are harvested plants, birds, animals, or fish; and finally, natural park areas that can be looked at but may not be touched.

Maybe this situation really is what some people would like to see. Decision makers, however, cannot act on such visions. They have to take reality into account. The fact is that there are considerable groups of people who live by hunting and fishing, and whose livelihood cannot be disposed of just like that. It is also important for decision makers to remember that these people are not willing to accept any form of compromise in the matter of their fundamental right to hunt and eat sea mammals. Even to question this right they consider a declaration of war.[13]

At another level, too, a war is going ont. Everyone who has seen the repulsive videos of the tuna fisheries in the eastern Pacific Ocean knows that here, as well, a war is being waged against nature, with the single objective of creating more profit and still more profit.

Until recently, it was the big whales that had to pay the price for this kind of warfare. Only one question was asked by the capital-intensive whaling companies: "Is it profitable?" If there was any concern about the well-being of the stocks, it was swept aside. But the pendulum swung to the other side, the public developed a guilty conscience, and the big antiwhaling campaigns threw their weight behind the massive change of attitude that has now made it a mortal sin to hunt even a single large whale, whether or not the species in question is endangered. In the course of a decade public opinion swung from one extreme to another.

Are we not confronted with the same pattern in regard to the small cetaceans? Will the pendulum swing from one extreme to the other in this matter as well?

In the IWC there has been a debate for many years about whether or not the commission is competent to decide management principles not only for large whales but also for the smaller ones, in other words, to decide on quotas and hunting methods for all toothed whales, from the killer whales on down. It is a divisive issue.

An important segment among opinion makers—inspired by the protectionist nations—agrees that the IWC should have authority over all kinds of whales, big as well as small, whether they have baleen or teeth. Other countries are of the opinion that the IWC's competence is limited to the species list that was promulgated by the Whaling Convention of 1946, which includes only the large whales. What might seem a purely bureaucratic battle over words is in reality a question of how much national jurisdiction the member countries are ready to cede to this international organ, the IWC.

The problems connected with small cetacean mortality worldwide, intended and unintended, have never been compiled any single place. This issue has a whole series of implications—socioeconomic, cultural, industrial, and legal—which vary greatly from one country to the next. None of the IWC member countries are opposed to scientific analyses of the biological status of the species and stocks inside their territories, but many are reluctant to give the IWC the authority to open the Pandora's box of some imaginary global management regime for the small whales. There is not much general confidence that this forum would be able to pass reasonable judgments or regulate worldwide such a maze of intricate national and local issues.

In the Arctic the beluga and the narwhal are in focus, but also the pilot whale (well known from the Faroe Islands) and the ubiquitous harbor porpoise. In this part of the world, where vegetables cannot grow, these small whales function as an important source of food and—not the least significant element—vitamin C. Rules governing the harvest of these animals originate largely at a local level and go back many generations. In the Faroe Islands, written evidence of such rules extends all the way back to the Middle Ages. There is an unshakable confidence in the small communities throughout the Arctic that the small whales, highly prized as they are, are as well managed today as they have always been, and people resent the patronizing intrusion in their affairs by what they see as know-it-alls from the dominant societies to the south. After all, colonial times are said to be over.

In Greenland, where beluga and narwhal hunting is essential to the municipalities of the High Arctic, this entire matter amounts to a constitutional issue with Denmark. Greenland entered the IWC when Denmark signed the Whaling Convention of 1946. Greenland was a Danish colony at the time, and in no position to ask impertinent questions. When, in 1979, political autonomy was introduced (i.e., a self-governing status in matters concerning, among other things, wildlife and natural resources), Greenland had been an IWC member of a sort for thirty-three years, and chose to continue the membership. There was a clear understanding that only the big whales would be regulated by IWC quotas.

As it is, Denmark remains a member of the IWC, and the two autonomous Danish dependencies, the Faroes and Greenland, accept representation by the Danish government in the matter of big

A polar Eskimo from Thule, Greenland, after landing a beluga. October 1985. (Photo by Mads Faeg-teborg, Copenhagen)

whales. Management of small cetaceans as a political matter was transferred to the Faroes in 1948 and to Greenland in 1979. The Greenlanders and Faroese are adamant that nobody is able to manage the small cetaceans better than they are. Increased international pressure on the Danish government to change this state of affairs can only lead to more useless and ill-tempered political rhetoric in an already very hot debate. Denmark possesses no authority, either legal or moral, to change anything. It is in a bind.

This part of Denmark's situation is probably difficult to understand for the English-speaking countries that function as scoutmasters of the protectionist camp. They have never themselves had the "problem" of having to treat aboriginal peoples as equal. They have always been able to push and punch their minorities into place, especially the more exotic ones. The dominant Anglo-Saxons in the United States and the United Kingdom, in one hemisphere, and Australia and New Zealand, in the other, clearly believe that their place is on the moral high ground and that they are in a position to tell the rest of the world how things should be done—in the particular matter at hand, what kind of relationship between animal and man is ethically acceptable. What people on the Faroe Islands and in Greenland have to say about the self-righteous missionary attitude spread by the Anglo-Saxon-dominated environmental movements is not fit to print.

The opposition to turning authority over the small whales over to an international forum has not, on the other hand, led to any general antipathy toward cooperation with other countries. The Greenland Home Rule authorities are perfectly willing to undertake bilateral research and management agreements that are in the interest of all concerned. Thus, in 1989, Greenland entered into an agreement with neighboring Canada to cooperate formally in the safeguarding and management of the narwhal and beluga. An expanded common research program was also agreed upon at that time. The background to this agreement is the traditional use by hunters in both Greenland and Canada of small cetaceans in the Davis Strait, Baffin Bay, and the Thule district.

There can be no doubt that in the coming years, we stand to experience an extraordinarily uncomfortable conflict over the management of the small cetaceans worldwide. Like the large whales, they mobilize the "oceanic feeling." They assume an increasingly symbolic connotation for the environmental movement at large. They manage to make many people feel guilty about the shameless race for profit that destroys nature's living resources as if it were an exercise in strip mining. And then the pendulum swings: because the industry massacres and throws away hundreds of thousands of dolphins in order to carry out the tuna fishery, which is so profitable, because innumerable small whales suffocate in industrial waste and are killed in huge drift nets for no reason at all, therefore the traditional hunt on small whales, which in itself has never endangered the species or represented any great waste, is suddenly thrust into the limelight.

The logic is muddy, yet seems to be emotionally compelling: because the industrial way of life is antinature, nature has to be protected against everyone—even against those who do not threaten it.

Ethics of a Killer Whale

Nobody who has followed the whaling/antiwhaling debate over the last few years can be in doubt: as the IWC Scientific Committee is able to report more and more whale stocks in good health, and as the work on a revised set of management procedures for resumed whaling activity nears its completion, the antiwhaling lobby has begun to lean increasingly toward a moral line of reasoning. Whales are intelligent and sentient, this group argues; they are wonderful and very special creatures, and it is quite simply immoral to kill them. A whole new series of arguments is being used to exempt whales from the general regime of sustainable use of nature's resources. We are all being told to stop thinking of humans as something special: whales too are unique, and we should beware of thinking along the lines of familiar anthropocentric morality.

This new line of thinking is a challenge to traditional ethics. In Western and Middle Eastern faiths—Jewish, Christian, Islamic—it is presupposed that biological life appears in two categories: humankind and all the rest. Humans alone are made in the image of God.

The Darwinian perspective presents biological life as a continuum, but with built-in mutations that lift it into different and progressively higher levels. With the awakening of consciousness of the self, combined with the ability to speak, the human being became the first and so far the only animal capable of pointing a finger, saying "you" and "I". Thereby humans reached a stage of life essentially different from that of all other life manifestations. The foundation was laid for a conscious individualization process inside the species of *Homo sapiens*.

In all other animal species, survival mechanisms are geared, in the end, to the survival of the group, the population, the species. In situations of stress, most vertebrate animals fend for themselves and their progeny, obviously with no thought for the species, but in this way the interests of the species are served. No animals other than humans have passed the threshold of individualization, where, in situations of stress, the interests of the individual can be brought to militate against those of the group. With the advent of *Homo sapiens*, a level of evolution was reached where it became reasonable and proper to start caring consciously for the individual, indeed, in some respects valuing the individual above all—the individual *Homo sapiens*, that is, not the individuals of other animal species.

Historically, this phenomenon has been most apparent in the thought of the great religious personalities throughout the ages, all stressing the immense value of each single human person. In relatively modern history, as we know, this idea has received collective and societal support with the French Revolution, the American Declaration of Independence, and—in our own times—the UN Charter of Human Rights.

Humans are the only animals to make the distinction between good and evil, and unlike other animals, humans are continuously exploring all possible facets and extremes of both good and evil, putting acceptable behavioral codes to a constant test. We will always have among us a Dr. Mengele and a Mother Teresa. This process doesn't go on without a lot of noise, involving both heroism and tragedy. Only humans are capable of heroism and tragedy on an individual, personal basis. We are restless and probing, and unlike other animals we are obviously ill at ease with ourselves, capable of behaving humanely as well as inhumanely. It is no foregone conclusion that we will be at harmony with our inner selves.

Not so the other animals. There is no evidence whatever that they feel anything like remorse when hunting and killing one another. They know no good and evil: they are innocent. No whale can exhibit "unwhalely behavior"—not even a killer whale. At this level, a whale is like any other animal. This is part of the simplicity and the beauty of the animal world; this is part of what makes inhumane treatment of animals so unbearable: when abused, they are not only defenseless, they are quintessentially innocent victims of the evil whims or greed of humankind.

In our part of the world, this has, for millennia, been the fundamental view of the man-animal relationship. It still is, inasmuch as all formal lawmaking concerning rights and duties is centered on human beings.

Is this view becoming obsolete?

Granted, we have in front of us, every day, everywhere here in the West, evidence of a caricature of the Judeo-Christian model of the animals' role: the human being on top of creation, with the legally unchallenged right to destroy animal habitats, wage unnecessarily cruel wars against pest animals, toxify the food chain, and enslave so-called domestic animals by the millions, if not billions, for industrialized execution. In other words, there is seemingly unlimited abuse. Then, in all fairness, we also have many examples of responsible and reasonable management of animal life, whether domestic or wild. But the fact remains that animals do have problems with humans—bad problems.

Obviously, there are two ways we can attack this issue: either by stressing *our duty as humans* to behave ethically vis-à-vis the animals or by talking about *the right of the animals* to be treated reasonably.

The first approach to the problem is consonant with traditional Western thought. According to the best of this tradition, we cannot just heedlessly destroy animal habitats or inflict wanton loss and suffering. We have an obligation to treat all of creation right. Whether we like it or not, we are in actual fact stewards of the nature of which we are the masters.

Over and against this view, the second approach is now emerging: that of animals having rights. Humans are not that special after all, it is said, and have no reason to feel conceited. Biological life is a continuum from the least evolved form to the highest. If we think that humans have a right to live insofar as possible without suffering, we must perforce grant that right also to other species than our own, inasmuch as they too are capable of pain. Any creature capable of pain has a right not to be subjected to unnecessary suffering. Any talk about a special ethical prerogative in favor of humans is not only nonsense, it is an especially foul kind of species-based narrow-mindedness and chauvinism: it is *speciesism*. Peter Singer, the Australian philosopher who has originated most of the contemporary animal-liberation thinking, mentions the theoretical example of a medical experiment that must be performed on a living animal. If the scientist in charge has access to a mentally retarded person, he argues, the experiment could just as well be performed on her or him rather than on a healthy, sentient rat.[14]

One point in this line of reasoning, however, is not properly elucidated. In the ethical standards governing our day-to-day behavior, rights are intimately connected with duties. If you have a human right to democracy, then you also have an obligation—a moral obligation, not necessarily a juridical one—to behave democratically yourself. If you have the right to know the truth, you also have the duty to be truthful yourself. If animals have their rights, what are their duties?

Does it make sense to talk this way in the first place? Duties presuppose an ethical standard. Do animals have an ethic? What is the ethic of a killer whale?

Clearly, this question is devoid of meaning. Animals can have no obligations of any ordinary sense of the word. They make no moral choices.[15] They are simple and innocent and at peace with themselves, even when they hunt and kill one another. If you want to attribute the concept of "right" to animals, which intrinsically and at all times are incapable of assuming duties, then the word *right* assumes a different meaning. Presumably, the only purpose of this exercise is to translate the whole matter into an obligation for humans to treat animals correctly—an obligation that was there anyway in the first place.

Animal-rights proponents, dealing with the specific question of whales, argue that biological life comes in three categories: humans, whales, and all other animals and other biological life. Whales are a category apart because in the eyes of many people, they are uniquely special. "Other animals" are all other species placed below humans and whales in the respective food chains of land and sea.

This view may have been most clearly forwarded by Robbins Barstow.[16] Dr. Barstow doesn't make use of the general animal-rights rhetoric. He argues the cause of the whales and nothing else. As far as the basic relationship between animals and humans goes, he doesn't forward any arguments against the sustainable use of nature's resources in general; he makes no distinction between the plant and animal kingdoms, and thus doesn't promote the vegetarian cause; neither does he argue against a sustainable and ecologically sound harvest of wildlife. His sole concern is the whales, for which he has a deep-seated feeling of wonder and awe. These strong emotions are motivated by a series of reasons—biological, ecological, cultural, political—which make him consider the whales uniquely special and therefore exempt from the general regime of sustainable utilization of wildlife as forwarded by the World Conservation Strategy and the Brundtland Commission Report.

Of course whales are a wonder of nature in very many ways,

and people are entitled to strong emotions about them. It seems, though, that there could be grounds for asking a few counter-questions: Are these views really as universal as some claim? Are they shared by the majority of the more than 1 billion Chinese, the 650 million people of Africa, the 80 million Arabs? Granted, we all know about public opinion in the Anglo-Saxon countries. But can one equate an Anglo-Saxon and, to some extent, Western European trend with world opinion?

In some countries, respect for an animal and the killing of it go together. In other countries, the two are opposed. To each of these types of culture, the attitude of the other is incomprehensible.

We all know that the Anglo-Saxon countries have a strong tradition of wanting to export their own cultural patterns and value systems to everybody else, and so it comes as no surprise that an essentially Western urban phenomenon is presented as "all but universal." But some questions must be asked: if cultures do exist in which respect for an animal and the killing of it go together, are they not entitled to go on existing? If not, what is the ethical reason for liquidating these cultures? If respect for an animal and the killing of it are mutually exclusive, what then is the attitude of Anglo-Saxon city dwellers toward the cows, pigs, and chickens in their own slaughterhouses? And what are the ethical grounds for this attitude, presumably one of contempt?

While never doubting for a moment that whales are uniquely special to many people, there is good reason to point to horses as very special to many other people. Are there fewer people to whom horses fall into this category than there are people to whom whales assume this role?

To the 670 million Hindus of the world, it's the cow that is truly special and sacred. Are there more than 670 million people in the world to whom a whale is more special than a cow? Maybe. It would be interesting to see the claim documented.

To the Arabs, the most divine of all creatures is the white gyrfalcon of the Arctic. They use it for their traditional hunting sports. They have a hard time getting hold of this bird, and they go to great lengths to procure it. In the Arab world, one gyrfalcon is surely valued more highly than many whales.

Or consider the eagle. This fascinating bird has qualified as the symbol of all imperialistic Western empires since the Romans.

Finally, to very many people around the world, the most special animal is the dog. Humankind's most ancient and faithful friend has lived from pole to pole, on all continents, at all times. This is by all counts the most useful, probably the most time-consuming, and certainly the most beloved of all animals. It lives with us in a symbiosis of unchallenged mutual enrichment, to use the term that Dr. Barstow applies to the relationship between whales and humans. What would all the lonesome folk, the watchmen, the shepherds—what would all the blind people of the world do without dogs? How would the entire Eskimo culture have come about without dogs? There can be no doubt: the dog is the most uniquely special of all animals. And yet, in some countries, people eat dogs. In Greenland we do, occasionally. Is there an *ethical* reason for not eating dogs—one that holds water philosophically?

The most serious objection against setting the seventy-nine whale species apart from the general regime governing animals and people is the fact that different times and different cultural circumstances produce different totem animals. Once you have decided to set whales apart in a politically different management regime because of your and your friends' personal emotional preferences, then there is no rational reason in the world to stop at the whales. Other people have feelings for other kinds of animals.

The process is simply bound to slide into the more general animal-rights philosophy. The seals, sea lions, and sea elephants are surely as brainy and wonderfully adapted to their environment as at least one or another of the many whale species, and so they too are entitled to a special regime. Otherwise we would be facing some kind of speciesism in favor of whales! If all marine mammals enjoy these special rights, then why not the semiaquatic animals? If beavers, what about all other furbearers in the woods? And so on, and so on. There is no doubt: if whales have rights, then every other sentient animal in the world with a brain capacity of some kind must have similar rights. Nothing else is philosophically consistent.

It cannot be a matter of moral rights, since animals can't be held morally responsible for anything. It will have to be a question of bestowing juridical rights on animals, their different nature notwithstanding, just as human rights are promulgated by the Human Rights Declaration of the United Nations. A political decision will have to be made about the right of animals to the pursuit of life and happiness according to the nature that is theirs.

Astounding as it is, this line of thinking does have its supporters—astounding if for no other reason than that it is completely impossible to put it into practice in any consistent way.

Whatever the animal-rights proponents may assert in support of their cause, the simple fact remains that any value system of any practical use perforce has to be human-centered. It is simply impossible to bestow on animals the same right to life and pursuit of happiness as we do on humans. The entire debate over the environment and the relationship between humans and animals is a struggle over space on a crowded planet. People multiply and proliferate from pole to pole as no other large-size mammal has ever done, from the mountains to the plains and far out at sea, everywhere. Animals are pushed away or forced into new patterns of ecological balance or imbalance. And we are being forced to do a lot of new thinking about our relationship with nature.

Through all this, one basic fact remains: no human group has ever been ready, so far, to sacrifice lives of its own in order to serve the interests of animals in jeopardy. Instead, humans always have been, and presumably always will be, ready to sacrifice the lives of the animals. This is the people-centered reality, and no responsible authority is about to change it. The world is crowded, and lives, both animal and human, have to be managed; but the difference is that all agree that policies of containment vis-à-vis human lives should be based upon birth control and family planning, whereas nobody disputes that animal population growth, when it is bothersome to humans, must be regulated through lethal measures. Anyone wanting to build a workable ethic for the relationship between humans and animals will have to take this simple fact into account, because it is not likely to be changed in any foreseeable future. Pest control is not unethical; on the contrary, it is clearly a moral act to curb the proliferation of disease-carrying rodents, to take just one obvious example. In any big city in the world, this control is effected by the ceaseless killing of millions and millions of rats by slow-working poison. Any big city is built upon a horrendous sea of suffering among this intelligent and sentient, family-loving but unfortunate, animal species. That is a terrible thought, yet it is a true one. But this killing is not unethical. It is a necessity.

Animal ethics will always be people-centered, for two reasons:

—ethics originate in the human mind, humans alone having a moral choice, and

—in a situation of conflict, human life will be preferred over animal life.

Once that has been said, there is every good reason to repeat what was pointed out earlier: that we are obliged to treat our fellow creatures right, protect their habitats, combat contamination of the environment, prevent harassment of animals, and avoid unnecessary cruelty in wildlife management and harvest practices. Humans must care.

Animals have no responsibility, either for good or for bad. They have no ethical standards. The killer whale does no evil when it teaches its young ones how to play cat and mouse with a stunned sea lion, or when it tears up an intensely suffering, defenseless humpback whale and starts eating off its tongue without bothering to kill it first. This is the cruel order of nature, and that cruelty is not evil. The killer whale is innocent.

We are not innocent. We are responsible. Killing animals can be legitimate, even necessary. But to us, wanton cruelty is evil. Unlike animals, we do know concepts like love of our fellow creatures and compassion.

We are under the obligation to care.

Cease Fire?

Everyone having an interest one way or another in the debate concerning whaling can confirm that it is wide-ranging, complex, strongly polarized, at times confusing, and often heated. It is what we call *politically sensitive*. At the center of the controversy, one question stands out: is it in our day and age at all acceptable to hunt and kill seals and whales? There are many who are against the practice, who argue that seals are cute and whales are intelligent. It is unpopular to kill wild animals. And there are many who really do believe that all seals and whales are threatened with extinction and who feel that it is a mortal sin to raise any weapon against them. Would it honestly be better to cease hunting them forever?

No, *not at all*. On the contrary: it would be a major sin to give in to this muddy wave of emotionally charged misinformation.

It is vital that coastal and island nations use and control the resources of the seas, just as the agricultural nations control four-footed animals, tame or wild. Whether the animal lovers of the cities like it or not, the fishing nations have always competed with seals and whales for fish. If they want to control one end of the food chain—and they have to!—they must control the other end as well, and this often means a certain measure of hunting, just as the European farmers must control deer (by shooting them) in order to protect their crops, and the American ranchers must control coyotes (by trapping them) in order to protect their cattle or sheep. This is the way it is, and who can change it?

Even more important is the nutritional aspect. In the Arctic, seals and whales are hunted and killed for food, together with sea fowl, caribou, musk ox, and fish. Take away people's right to hunt and kill for food, and they will have no other option than to leave their country and move—but where?

Unbelievable as it may sound, this "solution" is being proposed not only—as one might expect—during heated debates between humane societies and native organizations, but even in a prestigious magazine like the *American Journal of International Law*.[17] In an article about the "whales' right to life," two American lawyers propose that the Inuit stop whaling and "migrate to places where food is more plentiful, or set up arctic farms."[17] What exactly the two authors have in mind by "arctic farms" remains nebulous, but their intention of depopulating the Alaska North Slope and a major part of the Canadian Arctic, as well as all of eastern and northwestern Greenland, is rather clear. This is where people subsist on marine mammals: seal, walrus, and whales big and small.

Two academics writing in a law journal do not, of course, represent U.S. policy. In the IWC meeting in Reykjavik, Iceland, in May 1991, the U.S. delegation clearly announced the government's intention to honor all reasonable claims of the remaining Eskimo culture, including the right to hunt a limited number of the Bering Strait bowhead, which, despite the claim made in the *American Journal of International Law*, is not a threatened species.[18] The official U.S. policy must be a responsible one and cannot be dictated by emotions about what kind of life-style Native Americans ought to adopt, including what kind of food they should eat.

Antiwhaling sentiment, as it is filtered through the officialdom of the various national delegations to the IWC, is not directed against aboriginal subsistence whaling. Alaskan Eskimos and Greenland Inuit have been treated in the IWC in a positive way so far. The campaigns are directed against large-scale industrial whaling, and with good reason. After all, it was the whaling factory ships that brought the blue whale to the brink of extinction and threatened a number of stocks of other large whale species.

This battle, however, *has been won*. There *are* no more large factory ships engaged in whaling operations aimed at vulnerable stocks or species. As a matter of fact, large-scale factory-ship whaling is subject to a moratorium all its own, which was enforced years before the general moratorium on commercial whaling.[19] Nobody in aboriginal whaling communities wants to hunt whales for soap, fertilizer, lubricants, glue, or anything similar. The whaling communities want *food*, and only sustainable harvests from abundant stocks, thoroughly monitored and controlled by international science.

However, if the species and stock have been proved to be thriving, as is the case with, for example, the North Atlantic minke whale, if the harvest level is acknowledged to be sustainable and is subjected to international scientific control, if the hunting techniques are humane, ensuring death within a few minutes from when a whale is struck, and if a coastal community wants to put whale meat on its tables, honoring these conditions, then there is only one reason to refuse permission: the desire to accommodate political constituencies in the dominant societies, where the very idea of eating whale meat is distasteful.

The whale war is not only a struggle to save threatened whale species and a fight against profit maximizing at the expense of the whales. It is also, at the other end of the spectrum, a struggle for the right to put on the dinner table whatever one pleases, as long as it is taken from species and stocks in good shape. To the Inuit and the coastal communities of the North, it is a struggle to defend a way of life and a culture close to the sea and all the good creatures from the deep.

It is from this perspective that we must view the International Convention for the Regulation of Whaling of 1946, which is acceded to by all the nations that show up at the IWC's meetings. The main objective of the convention is "to provide for the proper conservation of whale stocks and thus make possible the orderly development of the whaling industry." This *conservationist* goal of the IWC is clearly at odds with Australia's often-declared *protectionist*, no-touch policy, which has put not only that nation itself, but the entire

Finwhales in the Bay of Julianehaab, South Greenland (Narsaq Foto, Greenland)

Whaling Commission, in an awkward and unfair position. Being an adamant antiwhaling nation, why doesn't Australia just quit the whalers' club?

Or, from the opposite point of view, with Greenland's unalterable claim to wildlife harvest and subsistence whaling, which is irrelevant to the industrial objective of the convention, and which moreover is clearly at odds with the now-prevailing sentiment in the IWC, why don't the Home Rule authorities ask the Danish government to stop representing their interests in this antiwhalers' society? After all, Canada quit the club years ago, and Iceland is doing so now.[20] Those are Greenland's closest neighbors to the west and to the east, and Greenland is more dependant upon wildlife harvest than either of them.

But no, neither Australia nor Greenland is likely to quit the IWC. Australia hopes for a worldwide ban on whaling and stays for the purpose of undermining the basic aim of the convention. Greenland stays in the hope that the principle of sustainable harvest will win the day. After all, a lot of hard work was put into the IUCN's *World Conservation Strategy* and into the large Brundtland Commission Report, *Our Common Future*. As regards the issues under discussion here, the basic principles are crystal clear. There is no evidence to support the extension of a taboo over certain natural resources in favor of others, freeing some for exploitation and not others. The principle is *sustainability*. If a species or population can tolerate a certain degree of exploitation without significant reduction, there is nothing to hinder it; on the contrary. The Brundtland Commission Report expressly mentions the desirability of giving political strength to the vulnerable groups, typically the aboriginal groups who live directly off wildlife and the small coastal communities around the world whose entire livelihood is based on the living resources of the sea.[21]

All honor and respect are due to those who have rediscovered tenderness and love for our abused planet and who have prevented the extermination of the great whales. But let all respect and support also be afforded to those who wish to uphold humankind's age-old symbiosis with wild nature, and who in a responsible manner wish to preserve *Homo sapiens'* way of life throughout 98 percent of the time humans have been on the planet—the life of the hunter on land and at sea.

4 ✦ The Battle of the Traps

While the war against the seal hunt and whale hunt can be so termed only in a metaphorical sense, the trap war in fact looks like a genuine armed conflict. Planned according to a strategy whose goal is a total revolt against the structures of society, the trap war is waged against all use of fur, pelts, hides, and leathers, and it is fought against all use of animals for industrial or scientific purposes. Among the weapons are bomb attacks, arson, and fright campaigns in the most literal sense of the word. The war is waged against laboratories, furriers, and butcher shops. A completely new form of terrorism has come into being and is implanting itself in our society.

The hunter's old-fashioned steel trap has become for this movement the symbol of people's cruel abuse of animals. This exploitation has to stop, the movement's adherents argue, and from here they proceed to a revolt against the whole established human-animal relationship. Their vision is of a world in which we accept the same moral duties toward all living things as we do toward human beings. The movement is called animal rights, and its goal is the liberation of animals.

Life and Death

Just before Christmas 1988, a number of incendiary bombs exploded in several British department stores known for selling furs. At Harrod's in London, at Dingles in Plymouth, and at Howell's in Cardiff, there were extensive damages running into the hundreds of thousands of pounds. In four other department stores the bombs were discovered before they were detonated and were dismantled by the police's antiterrorist squads. At the same time several small

Trapper at work in the Canadian woods. (International Fur Trade Federation, Holte, Denmark)

bombs were sent by parcel post to a number of printers who produced brochures and sales advertising publications for the fur industry. A professor at Cambridge who worked on animal physiology was sent a letter bomb at his home address. An anonymous telephone call to the *Manchester Evening News* ascribed the responsibility to the ALF—the Animal Liberation Front.[1]

The Christmas bombings had an enormous impact on the British public, but they were not any great surprise for Scotland Yard. By November 1984 the Yard already had set up a special division whose only mandate was to keep an eye on the ALF. The division had been set up after a frightened public had been warned against buying Mars bars. A spokesperson for the ALF said that a number of the popular chocolate bars had been adulterated with rat poison because the company, Mars Confectionary, was paying for a scientific project that involved inducing tooth cavities in monkeys. An anonymous spokesperson from the ALF headquarters in London said to the press, "We do not care whether or not people die. Animals come first."[2] After the panic died down, it was decided that the warnings had probably been without substance. No adulterated Mars bars were ever found, but the impact of the threat was real enough for Scotland Yard to be mobilized.

Nobody but those directly involved knows how the ALF is organized. The movement has of course been strongly condemned from all sides, in numerous letters to the editor, editorials, and the British Parliament. The many moderate animal-protection societies in Great Britain are also ill at ease over the course that the animal-rights movement seems to be taking. They feel themselves discredited and are among those condemning the ALF. Nevertheless, the movement seems to be going ahead at full steam. Acts of terror continue to be carried out against the fur industry, against animal physiology labs at universities and hospitals, and against butcher shops. On 19 November 1984 the minister of the interior, David Mellor, reported to Parliament that a group of approximately twenty masked men had, on several occasions, broken into the private homes of scientists who used animals in their scientific work. They had forced them to sit with their hands spread out in front of them at their desks and then broken the bones in their hands with a sledgehammer.[3] Understandably, one can read in the British newspapers about scientists who no longer dare publish their research out of fear of the animal-rights terrorists.[4]

Terrorism works.

Butchers are sent innocent-looking letters with razor blades stuck into the corners.[5] Fur stores and hamburger restaurants have stones thrown through their windows.[6] Mink farms are attacked in the middle of the night and thousands of animals are "liberated" into the quiet English countryside.[7] And politicians who speak out against this kind of madness can be reasonably sure to lose their mandates in the next election.

The ALF motto is starting to be heard: "Meat is murder. Demonstrate to liberate. Learn to burn." Scotland Yard tracks ALF members, but so far the police have always arrived after the act. A new Battle of Britain is well under way, and nobody can doubt which way it is going. In England it is not only looked upon as immoral, it is downright dangerous, to walk around wearing a fur coat.

It is only by sheer luck that these acts of terrorism have not so far taken any human lives. In 1986, the ALF claimed responsibility for sixteen bomb attacks. In 1989 the number had risen to forty-four. The ALF used to market its message by means of incendiary bombs, but now the organization has started to use plastic explosives. On 6 June 1990 a car bomb exploded under a jeep belonging to a veterinary surgeon who worked at the Ministry of Defense's chemical and microbiological research center near Salisbury. She saved her life by throwing herself through her car window. Five days later the target was a colleague at the university in Bristol, also by means of a car bomb. This veterinarian also escaped, but his thirteen-month-old son did not. He was severely wounded.[8]

Although Great Britain was the first place hit by this madness, we should not be blind to the fact that the concerns behind this campaign are infiltrating many other countries. Posters for synthetic fur are seen everywhere in the Paris subway stations, and in France there is a movement afoot to establish the Front pour la libération des animaux (FLA). In Germany and Great Britain anti-Semitism has been employed in service of the movement. The fur trade has been carried out primarily by Jewish merchants since the Middle Ages, when Jews were forbidden to own property and thus had to be able to carry their possessions in bundles on their backs. The connection of Jews to the furrier's trade is thus long-standing—and what do we find starting to surface now? We find advertisements such as one with a typically Jewish-looking gentleman showing a ladies' fur, with words alluding to the gas chambers.[9] This shameless anti-Semitism is now spreading inside the animal-rights movement. In Germany people who employ advertising like this aim at the basest sentiments of the public while at the same time systematically infiltrating various church groups.[10] They try to capitalize on the fact that, especially in Germany, the church has always represented the cultural focal point and established the moral agenda for the people. Now the agenda includes animal services of worship and the fight against all animal subjugation.

It probably will be no easy matter, however, to convince the

How would you like your fur, madam?
Gassed, strangled, trapped or electrocuted?

Help stop the unnecessary and
barbaric slaughter of millions of animals.
Don't buy a fur coat.

LYNX

FIGHTING THE FUR TRADE

The antifur organization Lynx is among the most aggressive of the animal rights groups that operate in full daylight. The group has been particularly active in lobbying the European Parliament. This controversial poster precipitated a lawsuit against Lynx for anti-Semitism. (International Fur Trade Association, Holte, Denmark)

churches—the Evangelical-Lutheran and the Roman Catholic—to join the antifur crusade. After all, it has never been a matter of doctrine that Jesus died on the cross so that animals could go to heaven. More important, the churches have always been for everyone, and they tend to be strongly conservative. Revolutions have seldom been sanctioned by the churches, and revolution is what the animal-rights movement wants.

Traps

For centuries people have caught wild animals in traps either for consumption or to protect their domestic animals or themselves. During many thousands of years traps have been set for bears, wolves, foxes, and martens, for mice and rats—even for the peaceful mole. It is never a pleasant experience for an animal to be caught in a trap. Among the most unsavory ones is the mole trap, which with jagged metal jaws hangs onto, squeezes, and mutilates the snout or neck of the mole, without any guarantee that the animal will die before the executioner gets there. The mole is classified as a pest animal because it upsets the gardener's aesthetic notions of well-ordered flower beds and beautifully leveled lawns.

Mole traps are used both in England, which is famous for its well-kept lawns, and also in orderly and meticulous Germany. But when the European Parliament's Intergroup for Animal Welfare starts a loud and outraged discussion of the mistreatment of animals and the barbarity of steel traps, the mole trap is never mentioned. No, the discussion concerns itself only with non-European animals such as the Canadian lynx, the North American beaver, and the Russian sable. The market for these products must be obstructed and destroyed, argue the proponents of the animal-rights movement, and trappers from the cold-weather countries should find something else to do, because the suffering of the poor animals is such a shame!

Nobody will dispute that animals suffer when they are caught in traps. But neither can it be disputed that, all in all, a wild animal that lives its entire life in freedom and ends its days spending some hours or a day in a trap before it is killed suffers less than much of the industrialized livestock bred under cramped conditions. For animal lovers in industrial society it is much easier to talk about an import ban against fur from wild animals trapped in some faraway country than it is to change the conditions for milk-fed calves in Holland, force-fed geese in France, or caged chickens in the United States. It is much easier, but is it fair?

Fair play demands that one know what one is talking about. As to the urban animal lovers, only a few of them really know the full story about the traps used by contemporary fur hunters: how they work, where, and in what way and for how long the animal suffers in the trap.

In order to get an overview of the situation, it is probably a good idea to keep the well-established distinction between the killing trap and the live-hold devices. Since time immemorial, hunters around the world have developed many different ways to catch animals— contraptions where a stone falls down and smashes the head of the animal, mechanical traps, camouflaged holes in the ground, nets, snares, and many other things. But the traps that have become the focus of discussion in recent years are the metal leg-hold traps that the Scottish, English, and French fur hunters brought with them as they started to spread across and hunt in the great forest of North America. These small, easily transportable, and extremely effective pieces of modern "technology" quickly became standard equipment among the Indians everywhere in the areas now called Canada and Alaska, just as the Indians learned to use rifles and new means of transportation from the white Europeans. This is why the debate over the steel-jawed leg-hold trap turns out to be so important to the Indians in Canada and Alaska, to many of the Inuit in the Arctic, and to the aboriginal people inhabiting the enormous expanses of Siberia.

The old-fashioned "toothed" leg-hold trap was not humane. In the worst of circumstances it could even be as cruel as our domestic mole trap. It was made to hold the prey, not kill it, and there are many examples of this trap mutilating the poor animal in its desperate struggle to regain freedom. Historians of the future will honor our generation for being the one that made up its mind to discard this inhumane contraption once and for all.

It is in Canada, the United States, and Siberia that the hunting and trapping of furbearing animals is the most widespread and has the greatest social and economic importance. And it is in Canada and the United States that the first attempts were made to find new methods.[11] Already by the 1920s an antitrap campaign was under way, sponsored in the United States by the National Anti-Steel Trap League and in Canada by the Association for the Protection of Fur-Bearing Animals (APFA) and the Canadian Association for Humane Trapping (CAHT). From that time on, the Canadian campaign took a constructive direction. On the understanding that in many places and for many reasons, trapping of furbearing animals is a necessity, a systematic study was undertaken in order to develop new and more humane types of traps.

Even before CAHT had made itself noticed, a Canadian fur hunter by the name of Frank Conibear had developed a new kind of steel trap, one designed to be as practical and easily transportable as the traditional leg-hold trap. The difference from the traditional leg-hold trap was that the Conibear trap was a killing device. This invention later led to a whole series of different steel traps that all shared the same characteristic: the prey scarcely realizes that something has gone wrong before it is killed.

*Grade school excursion to an exhibition arranged by the ATFC, the aboriginal trappers'
association in Canada. On the wall are three Conibear killing traps. The largest is for lynx
and wolverine, the two smaller ones for fishers. Also pictured are two long-spring killing
traps, so-called drowning sets for muskrat and beaver. The canlike contraption at the bottom
is an Ymer-trap, an instant-kill device intended for small furbearers such as mink and
marten. On top, to the right and to the left, a skin scraper and a handsaw.* (Aboriginal
Trappers' Federation of Canada, Cornwall, Ontario, Canada)

Conibear steel traps have become standard equipment in many
places, though at the same time work goes on to find constantly
newer and better types of traps. As a result of increased pressure
from the Canadian humane societies, the Federal-Provincial Committee for Humane Trapping (FPCHT) was created in 1973. It became a line item in the Canadian federal budget, and it was specifi-
cally given the mandate to examine the possibilities for a realistic
solution to the problems of humane trapping. The committee finished its work in 1981 with the recommendation that except in certain
unusual cases, as when dealing with large predators such as wolves
and bears, the goal should be to develop quick-killing traps. During
its period of operation the committee evaluated 348 different kinds
of traps, of which only 16 were declared humane, or at least poten-
tially humane.

The Fur Institute of Canada (FIC), based in Toronto, was established in 1983 to continue and expand the work carried out by the FPCHT. The FIC furthermore has a mandate to develop an educational program for trappers and to undertake a much-needed public awareness campaign. The technical objective of the Fur Institute is to work with the kinds of snares and traps that hold the animal without mutilating it.

Similar work has been carried out for several decades in the United States at the Woodstream Corporation in Pennsylvania. Woodstream is the world's largest producer of traps and is the originator of the rubber-lined trap, which is enjoying an increasing popularity. This is the so-called soft-catch live-hold trap.

In 1986 a Canadian parliamentary committee recommended that the FIC take the initiative in standardizing hunting and trapping laws throughout the Canadian provinces. The final goal, which now is within reach, was to harmonize all of Canada's regulations and laws concerning traps in order to make it a legal requirement that reasonably humane traps be used.

There is no doubt that in this regard Canada is the leading nation in the world. No other country comes even close to having carried out such research or has used comparable funds in any animal-protection question. It is Canada whose lead should be followed in this regard.

Political Turbulence

It is therefore no coincidence that a Canadian was chosen to lead Technical Committee 191 of the United Nations International Standardization Organization, the United Nations agency for international standardization of weights, measures, and industrial norms (ISO-TC 191). The ISO-TC 191 has to provide recommendations for internationally acceptable standards for humane traps, and it has already begun to play a central role in this regard. It has become the peg upon which the European Commission hangs its hat during the conflict that has been brewing for years between Canada and the European Parliament in Strasbourg.

It all started on 4 February 1988, when the British minister of commerce, Alan Clarke, submitted a proposal for study to a number of organizations. The recommendation was that all fur in Britain should be tagged so that the consumer could see whether the pelts came from a certain list of animals caught in leg-hold traps. This so-called cruelty tag was intended for products from animals anywhere in the world that either "mainly" or "often" were caught in such devices. In reality this stricture would of course mean that pelts even from farm-raised animals might be tagged, since nobody can see the difference between the skins from wild and farm-grown animals. The goal of the proposal was quite formally and openly to stop the import of pelts, especially from Canada, where the trapping of furbearing animals has been the main occupation for large population groups for hundreds of years.

The Canadian Parliament protested strongly, and finally Prime Minister Margaret Thatcher was threatened during her visit in Ottawa with the cancellation of a Canadian nuclear submarine order for which British companies were competing. The Canadians aired the possibility that they might let the order go to France instead of England. Mrs. Thatcher gave in, and Alan Clarke's ideas came to nought—at least for the time being.

But the idea resurfaced in the European Common Market. In July 1988, in the European Parliament in Strasbourg, the British proposed a new resolution on cruelty tagging of fur in Europe.[12] The matter was discussed intensely and circulated in the corridors. It went to the Environmental and Consumer Protection Committee, it was forwarded to the EEC Commission in Brussels, and it was also on the agenda of the Economic and Social Committee. The entire EEC machinery ground into motion, firmly pushed by the European Parliament's Intergroup for Animal Welfare.

In the spring of 1989 the commission formulated its stand.[13] Unfortunately for the intergroup, there had in the meantime been a changeover among the commissioners so that environmental and consumer-protection matters were no longer in the portfolio of the Conservative Britisher Clinton Davis but rather in that of the new environmental commissioner, Ripa di Meana, an Italian Socialist.

Di Meana tried to solve the conflict by approaching the United Nations. Any EEC regulation on fur imports would touch upon a strong and vested interest outside Europe. Several of the EEC's most-favored trade partners, such as the United States and Canada, not only had moral responsibility for whatever hunting methods were used but also had to carry the economic and social burdens brought about by a possible change of hunting and marketing patterns. What, then, could be more reasonable than to start examining what these countries were doing in order to solve the problems connected with trapping?

Work in the ISO-TC 191 is carried out by representatives of countries where trapping plays an important role. Members of the committee at the time, besides Canada, were the United States, Australia, Sweden, Finland, Germany, and Argentina, and another ten nations had observer status. All member countries of the Untied Nations are welcome to join.

The members of the committee have now agreed on the basic requirements that have to be fulfilled in order for a killing device or a live-hold trap to be termed humane. The framework accepted by the committee permits about three minutes from the moment the animal is caught in the trap until it is dead; this is the national standard in Canada. An additional condition is that the committee wishes to make sure that before it dies the animal becomes "irreversibly unconscious" as quickly as possible.[14] Furthermore, the committee plans to add a time limit for the final changeover from old-fashioned traps to the new ones.[15] A number of humane traps have already been developed and are being used, though others that have shown promise have to be improved in efficiency and practicality. Once these improvements have been made, further testing will be carried out in the field, and finally the results of these tests will be evaluated by the committee. This process may result in new demands from the member countries, new tests in the field, and new reports. All these things take time, especially since the practical testing has to take place during the specific and time-limited hunting seasons for the animal species in question, often only a few months a year.

Until recently, the working group's assumption has been that at best it will be 1996 before all the old-fashioned leg-hold traps have been changed for other and better models in the professional fur hunt in the major countries concerned. The optimists have therefore hoped that by 1996 there will be legal requirements in place that will please animal lovers—not to mention easing the deaths of the animals themselves—in the United States, Canada, Sweden, Finland, and possibly Russia. Others, probably more realistic, think that the year might be 1998. At that time, it can be expected that every wild animal hunted for the sake of its fur will be taken by licensed and educated professional hunters. It can also be expected either that the animal will be killed immediately when it is caught in the trap or that the trap is guaranteed to hold the animal without mutilating it or making it suffer.

Such is the excellent piece of work by the United Nations that inspired the EEC environmental commissioner to try to implement his European scheme. At an early stage the EEC Commission signaled that in this matter it was reasonable to accept and respect the United Nations' greater insight and competence, as well as responsibility. But what happened?

Influential members of the European Parliament's Intergroup for Animal Welfare did not want anything to do with this kind of approach. The motto seemed to be: "Do not disturb us with facts!" These people were high-profile politicians who did not want to be bothered with such "insignificant" details. They wanted cruelty tagging of furs. They fabricated resolutions in which old-fashioned leghold traps were mixed up with Conibear traps in one large pot of misinformation. They pronounced animal species endangered that are not anywhere close to that status. They wanted an import ban against pelts from countries that do not obediently bend their minds and turn their backs on their hunting traditions. The EEC Commission's original proposal for a time frame of 1996–1998, built upon the excellent work of the UN Standardization Organization, has been pushed aside, without any argument, as just too long a time period. The fact that it concerns the way of life and source of income of more than two hundred thousand Indians in Canada alone, and many thousands more in Alaska, they just couldn't be bothered to deal with. Those people surely must have a government to take care of their "problems," the argument ran, and as far as Canada goes, because it is such a rich country, why doesn't Ottawa simply provide more social welfare for the Indians? In short, just leave those animals in the forest alone![16] An invitation from one of the aboriginal organizations in North America, Indigenous Survival International (ISI), for intergroup members to come to Canada and look at the situation themselves was obstructed and delayed time after time ("Do not disturb us with facts!"). A delegation from ISI to London, Brussels, and Strasbourg was made to look suspicious and was kept on the sidelines as much as possible. Excitement and hysteria spread. The international media began to notice the controversy. The politicians, of course, wanted to be seen to be on the right side of the issue. None of them wished to lose votes in their constituencies over an issue of environment and animal welfare. That even the United Nations is involved in this case was overlooked in a loud silence.

On the other hand, inside the Intergroup for Animal Welfare itself, a power struggle was building up. The one-eyed leaders, some of them very influential, were encountering opposition from other members of the group. In the end, the majority of the group accepted the invitation from ISI. A delegation was sent to Canada, and their findings eventually managed to temper the Intergroup's recommendations.

Finally, in his proposal to the Council of Ministers, Ripa di Meana recommended that by 1995 there be an import ban against pelts and furs from a list of specific animal species in countries that have not exchanged all the old-fashioned traps for the newer, more humane ones. Furthermore, the proposal raises the possibility that countries with real and documentable problems in attempting to meet this deadline can obtain an extension until 1996.

Will the matter stop there? That remains to be seen. The antitrap people are on the warpath.

Artificial Fur

One person's pain is another person's gain. What you lose on the swings, you gain on the merry-go-round. Isn't that so? Whatever the political turbulence, something or other might still come from it.

Has the textile and the artificial material industry a vested interest in the disintegration of the natural fur market and, further down the road, the leather industry? Will skins and hides be pushed out of the food chain of commerce? Somebody in the business world must have such visions. How else do you account for all those ads for artificial fur in England, the United States, France, and Germany? There is money in everything and there is also money in the antitrapping protest industry. All those slogans about the way fur lovers are "just supporting capitalism" have an empty ring to them.

In the fall of 1989, proof surfaced of the chemical industries' interest in supporting the opponents of natural furs. The big English petrochemical textile firm Gore-Tex sponsored, during huge demonstrations in Trafalgar Square, "the definitive anti-fur campaign." It was the British animal-rights organization Lynx that, supported by

Brigitte Bardot in Inuit Country: "Couldn't your wife just use artificial fur like the rest of us?" (Drawing by Bo Bojesen, Politiken, Copenhagen, February 1978)

Gore-Tex money, undertook the mass campaign, which would have included public burning of natural furs had not the police intervened.[17] Gore-Tex is a waterproof material that is biologically nondegradable. As a part of this sales campaign, the fabric was championed by a number of sports people, models, and so on, who all pointed out that the products of the petrochemical industry, especially Gore-Tex, were better and more practical than fur and—above all—more environmentally correct and nature-oriented. Half a year later, after Lynx had fallen into disgrace among certain segments of the British public, Gore and Associates sent out a press release in which the company distanced itself from Lynx and other such special-interest groups by offering the remarkably honest explanation that its early sponsorship of Lynx's activities had been motivated only by the simple wish to sell more of its own products.[18]

It may well be true that there is lots of money to be made in the petrochemical textile industry, responds the public. But we do not want to run the risk of supporting the decimation of the wild animals that are left. The struggle to preserve nature and the environment in as unspoiled a condition as possible, everywhere, has to be everyone's overshadowing concern. And it can't be wrong to wear the many excellent synthetic textiles and artificial furs that are produced nowadays. Then at least one can be certain one is not endangering the environment.

Is that so?

Not only are natural products beautiful and appealing, but, more important, one day they disappear; they return to nature whence they came. Wood, paper, linen, cotton, silk, leather, and fur all finish their lives by dissolving into their various elements; they mildew, rot, or get worn out. They disappear back into Mother Nature's big storehouse. A natural product is part or the biosphere's perpetual self-renewing process, just like the human body itself, which starts as the natural products semen and egg and ends as food for the worms.

Artificial products cannot be recycled. They are anti-nature. Nature is biodegradable. But humans have now, so help us God, become capable of creating nonbiodegradable materials—nylon, polyester, acrylics, modacryl, teralyne, and whatever else they are called—which never rot or wear out and which we have to live with perpetually, however many times we throw them away. The oceans are filled slowly with old fishing nets and drift nets that float around, bothering or killing birds, seals, whales, and fish. Beaches and cliffs on the furthest islands, from the Pacific Ocean to the North Atlantic, are polluted slowly but surely by plastic bags and plastic bottles, nylon ropes and foam rubber—which *never* disappear. And it goes on and on, more and more, year after year. What will all this lead to? What will our earth look like in five hundred years, after twenty generations of pollution by all these products of antinature?

In August 1989 a sperm whale was beached in Conception Bay in Newfoundland. It was impossible to save it, and when a team of whale researchers examined its stomach contents they found, apart from the usual squid, twenty-seven different pieces of old fishing equipment and plastic garbage. The director of the biology team, Dr. Jan Lien, from Memorial University in Newfoundland, said that by now it has become commonplace to find in whale stomachs nylon rope, rubber boots, plastic bottles, whole or parts of fishing nets, and much more inedible junk that has been thrown overboard from ships. This kind of "junk food" is a very risky menu for a whale, Lien told *Fishing News International*; he suggested that fishermen think twice before they throw their garbage overboard into the sea.[19]

Trans-Alaska oil pipeline, near Fairbanks, Alaska. (Photo by Richard A. Caulfield, Fairbanks, Alaska)

Can we be certain we are not threatening the environment if we wear artificial fur? While we await the news about the humpback whale that suffocated on an environmentally correct nylon fur off New England's coast, maybe we can pass the time by philosophizing about what happens when you produce one of these repugnant anti-nature "furs."

It seems that nobody really knows what happens in the manufacturing process. We do know that these artificial materials are by-products from the oil and gas industries. Furthermore, it has been found that the process creates a number of chemical reactions so new and multifaceted that nobody, not even among the experts, has the foggiest idea how dangerous they can possibly be. We do know that most of the artificial materials are nonbiodegradable, and a number of scientists are convinced that to a considerable extent, these artifacts of chemistry represent a quickly growing family that is among the most dangerous of all hitherto-known environmental poisons. The family name is *dioxin*.

If you become scared by all this talk about dangerous materials and would like to get rid of your "chemical fur," then of course you

Young Siberian participants in the first Children of the Arctic festival. The headwear, from left to right, is made of arctic fox, white reindeer, brown reindeer, and red fox. Salekhard, Siberia. March 1991. (Photo by Mads Faegteborg, Copenhagen)

can just throw it on a bonfire can't you? There is absolutely nothing wrong with these materials' flammability.

No, that is exactly what you must not do! Acrylics, which are some of the most flammable artificial materials—in fact, they burn even better than oil—give off prussic acid when they burn. Artificial products that contain chlorine compounds are known to develop dioxins when they are burned at too low a temperature, such as on a bonfire in the open air. Apart from this, nobody really knows much about what happens during the uncontrolled burning of artificial materials, except that a number of environmental poisons seem to be given off, and that it will cost unacceptably large sums to have the matter fully researched. This is exactly why, for decades now, the Danish textile industry has fought private burning of textile waste, which usually contains a certain amount of artificial fibers. This kind of material is now either deposited in controlled garbage dumps, where it will stay for the bother and nuisance of people forever more, or driven to special incinerator plants, where the escape of dioxin is prevented by a special combustion procedure.[20]

Let nobody be in doubt. If they are not treated correctly, these are extremely dangerous products. The pollution they cause is so violent that it will shortly endanger the entire Arctic food chain. Already the first alarm bells have gone off among nutrition experts who are of the opinion that polar bear and walrus meat will have become inedible in a short while. What is going to happen to the Arctic peoples and their food culture?[21]

This is an almost apocalyptical perspective, and frightening even if it is only half true. What concerns us here, in this connection, is the artificial fur industry. Is it environmentally friendly and correct?

No, not at all; quite the contrary. It conducts a biased and misinformed witch-hunt against the use of animals. In its production processes it helps to pollute the world we live in, invisibly and dangerously. And about the product that hangs on the shoulders of many women nowadays we have to say the most awful thing that can be said about anything: it is totally indestructible, impossible to get rid of. The artificial fur is an unsolvable garbage problem as far into the future as anybody can see.

It is not right that we should promote such a miscreation. There is nobody who can surpass God's own product in beauty or environmental fitness.

Let us hold onto animal furs. At least we know what they are.

5 ◆ Which Way?

A Place for Wilderness People

A short while ago, approximately twelve thousand years or so, there was a major change in history. The genetic mutation *Homo sapiens neanderthalensis* had long since become extinct, and the human—*Homo sapiens sapiens*, the hunter and gatherer—was now present on the five continents of the earth.

Then somebody learned to sow and to harvest.

This innovation probably emerged in several places independently of each other, and long before agriculture as such was systematized.[1] It most notably emerged somewhere in what is now known as Iran or Iraq. Around this time the countries of the Middle East shaped world history as we know it. With the systematic introduction of agriculture, the nomadic life was marginalized. The village community played a new role, and power structures assumed new forms. Primitive agricultural techniques were developed and, as an accompaniment, an interest in technology as such. People started to specialize in certain occupations, and animals were domesticated.

Leisure time became a factor in people's lives, at least for the leaders and their protégés, and in a very short span of time the world changed completely. Now people didn't have to spend their time chasing gazelles with stone axes. There was time for art and for war. Metals were introduced. Intellectual life was formalized. The big religions were founded. Wars and power struggles took continuously new forms and rolled back and forth like giant waves over what by now had become many different groups of peoples and nations.

Towns were founded. A framework was set for a life-style that would alienate people from nature. Nobody, of course, had any idea where this aspect of the process would lead. It just happened, and today we are in the midst of the consequences.

The village culture brought a time of great controversies. It stands to reason that one of the first big conflicts had to do with the alienation of the herder of sheep and goats from the hunters' community. It comes as no surprise that it is from the Middle East that we first hear the echo of this conflict. Two or three thousand years ago a legend was committed to writing whose roots must have gone even further back, perhaps another couple of thousand years. It is the story about the twin brothers who were at odds even from their mother's womb. He who was born first was to become a hairy hunter roaming the wilderness; the other, a smooth-skinned husbandman leading a calm and well-organized family life. Even before they were born—so goes the story—their mother was given a premonition about her sons: "Two nations are in thy womb, and two manner of people shall be separated from thy bowels; and the one people shall be stronger than the other people; and the elder shall serve the younger."[2]

This prophecy has been fulfilled many times. In the biblical story about Esau and Jacob we recognize without any difficulty, step by step, the many tragic defeats that aboriginal hunters have suffered ever since they were first confronted with articulate busybodies who manipulated them out of their birthright, pushed them out of the way, cheated and repressed them. Do we need to retell the story of the North American Indians, to take one example known by every schoolchild? And further examples are legion in Australia, Latin America, the countries of the former Soviet Union, Africa, Southeast Asia, and Alaska. Hunting people have been pushed, pressed, marginalized, and massacred.[3]

Yet a countermovement has begun to grow. Indigenous people are organizing themselves, and that in itself is something new. On the international scene, we now see Arctic grass-roots organizations like the Inuit Circumpolar Conference (ICC) and ISI. We see their points of view in *Caring for the Earth*, the new edition of the World Conservation Union's strategy.[4] We hear their voices during meetings of the IWC and of the Washington Convention where the trade in commercial products of endangered species is monitored. We hear

Esau and Jacob: the relationship between bushmen and Zulus in southern Africa is a text-book example of the conflict between hunters and keepers of livestock. The Bushmen felt that the Zulus stole their hunting grounds. The Zulus, on the other hand, needed grazing land for their cattle, and they viewed the Bushmen as vagabonds and cattle thieves. This conflict often led to violent confrontations, as depicted here, as Zulus pursue a group of Bushmen escaping with cattle. (Kaj Birket-Smith, *Vi Mennesker*, Copenhagen, 1940)

them begging NATO to stop the destruction caused by low-level training flights of supersonic fighter jets in the big forests of Labra-dor, flights which frighten the wits out of everything alive, day and night.[5] We see them presenting themselves at the Parliament in Mos-cow with pleas for help against the industrial destruction of the Si-berian taiga and the habitats of the reindeer.[6] And they have learned the sophisticated political lobbying techniques of the European Par-liament in Strasbourg, presenting their case amid the noisy British, German, and Italian animal-protection groups, who couldn't care less about the survival of the last remnants of the North American Indian culture but want only to push through some uninformed antitrapping campaigns and appear as friends of nature in front of their just-as-uninformed constituents.

The indigenous communities around the world have made up their minds: they want to be heard.[7]

A Case in Point: The Eskimos and the American Way of Life

In 1962 a group of anthropologists and psychologists in Boston started an initiative whose goal was to improve the quality of instruction in geography and social sciences in American schools.[8] An experimental educational curriculum was developed, the cornerstone of which was to be anthropology as the starting point for comparative cultural studies. The idea behind it was to get the children to understand the relativity of cultures and to modify their prejudices about the superiority of the North American culture over other cultures. The project was funded by the National Science Foundation and the Ford Foundation.

Because it was thought that children in these television times could be reached most easily by means of film, the plan for the project was to film people of different cultures and present the films without any explanatory narrative or subtitles, so that the children's comprehension would depend only on the images and the actual sound—a process called naked representation. The children were to be placed "filmicly" on the scene, just as anthropologists would be, to become observers themselves and to draw their own conclusions. It was the consensus of the working group that by these means the students would achieve a greater comprehension of foreign cultures and thereby also a greater tolerance.

As the first subject, the Eskimo culture was chosen, the reason being the popularity of the Eskimos. Americans loved them, so it was said—those appealing people with a simple and easily understood way of life. The group in Boston contacted a Canadian group of anthropologists and film producers who were to film everything about the Netsilik Eskimos of the eastern Canadian Arctic. The plan was to show in detail what their life had been like before white people arrived—a reasonable goal in the case of the Netsilik people, to whom life before the intrusion of Western civilization was within living memory. They only started to use firearms in 1923.

The film project was sponsored by the National Film Board of Canada and came under the direction of the eminent and highly respected anthropologist Asen Balikci. The result was an extraordinary tour de force. After thirteen months' fieldwork in the Arctic under technically extreme conditions and the shooting of many hundreds of meters of footage, a series of ten films, each half an hour long, was finished. They showed practically every aspect of this Inuit community's original way of life. Even though it was the eleventh hour, the Netsilingmiut still knew how to function completely without modern weapons and tools. The films contained no pedagogical explanations; there was no translation of their very sparse commentary and no artificial background music or narrative. Only the natural sounds of the place and the people were in the films.

The group in Boston got a first-class product with which to start the new educational program. The films could not have been any better for the intended purpose. The group put together a program designed for the students in grade five, entitled "Man: A Course of Study" (MACOS). MACOS was distributed to three thousand elementary schools.

The reaction was unexpectedly strong and negative. The first opposition came from the parents. From there, the opposition quickly spilled over into the media, first the press and then radio and television. Now the politicians had a cause. The first responses came from the Bible Belt in the southern states, but it did not take long before protests arose all over the United States. On 11 May 1976 the matter appeared on the agenda for Congress in Washington, where one member of Congress from Arizona said: "MACOS is a subtle but sophisticated attack on Judaic-Christian family values. . . . embedded in the MACOS material is an 'anything goes' philosophy which subtly unteaches morality, patriotism, American values, Judaeo-Christian ethics and beliefs, so that children will be more accepting of a world view rather than an American view. . . . The exaggerations of the media have always been moderated by the use of black and white and by narrated interpretations, both of which remove the viewer from actuality and offer a point of view. The new films are in vivid color and are silent. . . . Every day it is violence and death."[9]

Of course, it had never been the intention to unteach good morals or national American values. Rather, the idea had been to imprint upon the children that healthy and reasonable patriotic feelings could very well coexist with a tolerance for alternative ways of life. Nobody, however, could contradict that the films' naked representation of Eskimo life was more vivid than ordinary media portrayals. It had been the intention from the outset to make the films in this way. The consequences were swift: the economic support was cut;

Zacharie and Martha Itimangneq, who played a key role in the realization of the great ethnographic project of the National Film Board of Canada. Pelly Bay, N.W.T., 1964. (Photo by the author)

the National Science Foundation pulled back; and the project fell apart.

For the anthropologists who were behind this fiasco the questions had to be, Why did it turn out this way? And why did nobody anticipate this result? In order to try to find some answers to these questions, a questionnaire was given to schoolchildren from the third to the ninth grades with the purpose of discovering why the Eskimos are so popular among American children. The results of the questionnaire showed that Eskimos are well liked because of several perceptions about them:

1. They live surrounded by snow. Their surroundings are white and completely clean, and Eskimos are consequently very *clean* people.

2. Their hunters are *courageous*; they can on their own deal with the most dangerous of wild animals, and they are not afraid of strong snowstorms.

3. Both men and women are *extremely hardworking* people who never sit still; they are always doing something useful.

4. They are very *inventive*; they live in difficult surroundings and survive with few means.

5. They are *good parents*; they love their families and take good care of them.

6. They are *generous*; they share their food with their neighbors.

7. They are *democratic and free* people; they are all equal and have no kings or tyrants above them.

8. They are *peace-loving*; they don't fight among each other and do not know war.

9. They are *honest*; they do not steal food from their neighbors.

The rationale behind these answers is easy to see. In the Inuit, American children had found an indigenous people upon which they could project their own society's traditional ideals. Americans regard the Inuit as a kind of primitive pioneers with strong and solid puritan virtues. But with MACOS, the children got a series of videotapes that destroyed all their preconceptions. During the Netsilingmiut's summer hunts, the Inuit turned out to be bloodthirsty wild men who thrust their harpoons into a swimming caribou. What were they doing to *Bambi*? And in technicolor, without explanations!

It is true that the everyday life of these people is full of blood and death, namely, that of the animals. American children's everyday television life, with its endless violence and crime, is also full of blood and death, but this the Arizona congressman did not see, and to him it was not relevant. After all, that is only human blood, and it is only for entertainment. Children are not harmed by that, or so argue some people in the United States.

The prejudices against hunting peoples and their symbiotic relationship with nature seem entrenched, not only in the United States but in all urban civilization. Where will these prejudices lead us all?

The Human Odyssey

The human being is quite a young animal. As a species we are only half a million years old. That is by itself only a fraction of the time when there have been two-legged industrious creatures on our earth. During these five hundred thousand years, human beings have become one of the world's most dangerous predators. Humans have been able to adapt themselves to every region and every climate, from the pole to the equator, much to the disadvantage of other animals. This ability is not shared by any other living being—perhaps with the exception of the common fly.

Human beings have not been kind to other creatures. If animals could speak, and if a meeting were called in a "parliament of animals," the first point on the agenda would most certainly be the containment of the destructive animal *Homo sapiens*.

If success is measured by the ability to reproduce, then *Homo sapiens*, in this very short time on earth, has shown itself as the greatest biological success of all time. There has never existed any other large mammalian species on the earth so numerically extensive. The fertility of humans is so great that our reproductive ability is now our biggest problem.

The human is the only conscious animal. This fact has not provided much peace of mind; rather the contrary. In the old days it was said that it was because of the fruit on the tree of knowledge of good and evil that our first ancestors lost their paradise. Nowadays human beings are not even at peace with their food. No other omnivorous animal has as many and as varied worries about whether it should

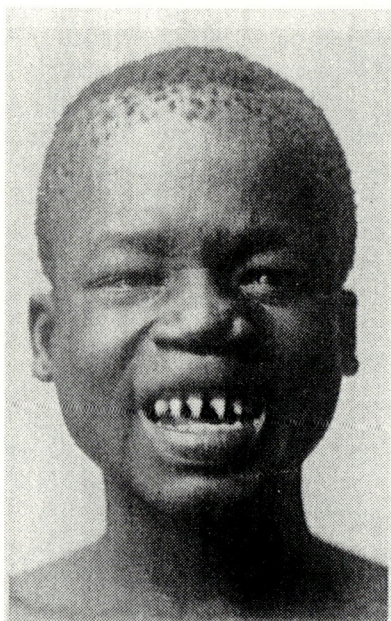

Our unique capacity for abstractions influences the way we conceive of our teeth. In some parts of Central Africa, sharp and pointed teeth are considered the ideal. In Western cultures, on the other hand, canines reveal the demon. (Photo reproduced with permission from Cambridge University Museum of Archaeology and Anthropology.)

eat this or that and why or why not. Consciousness about the origin, kind, and significance of food creates problems that no other animal has to deal with.

Our omnivorous nature is evidenced by our teeth. We have the molars of the vegetarian and the sharp canine teeth of the predatory animal. The latter are not particularly prominent, but they are there. To some peoples, sharp predatory teeth have been the ideal; their teeth were filed to achieve this effect. In other cultures, such as ours, the predatory teeth are looked upon as demoniac. The inner split in humans is such that they cannot even agree among themselves whether the shape nature has given their teeth is good or evil.

What strange animals we are!

The growth of the major religions that began three to four thousand years ago, with the collective and intense consciousness-raising they produced in humans, did not make things any easier. Food taboos were formalized and justified. In some places in the world, ideas about reincarnation resulted in an opposition to eating animals and led to vegetarianism. In other places, people had apocalyptic visions about a world order where "the wolf . . . shall dwell with the lamb, and the leopard shall lie down with the kid. . . . the cow and the bear shall feed [together] . . . and the lion shall eat straw like the ox."[10] In our times, it is possible to buy vegetarian cat and dog food at the British Vegetarian Society, if we would like to protect our pets against their "evil" instincts and help them on the road to cosmic harmony.[11] Isaiah did not live in vain, so it seems.

In many places in the world, human beings are liberated from their daily dependence on domestic animals. The interdependence between people and domesticated animals goes back to the era when agriculture was introduced, some ten thousand years ago. Now, in our day and age, we have witnessed a considerable alleviation of the daily work load of both animals and people. Wherever industry and technology make their way into society, life becomes less physically burdensome to all.

But mark it well: those same industries create enormous pollution that is destructive to animal habitats around the world. What is one to think of a society where people talk about the liberation of animals while—as a precondition for this exercise—destroying the living conditions for animals far and wide?

On the one hand, the industrial life-style undermines the very conditions for a healthy natural environment, and on the other hand, we are all witnessing an increasing demand that nature be left untouched. People's attitudes seem to be undergoing pendulum swings in a manner never seen before. Human beings have become almost schizophrenic in their attitude toward nature. In their guilty consciences over their own way of dealing with the earth, some urban folk turn vicious when faced with those who live in nature and use it sensibly—but with the best of intentions, of course![12]

The old baron Münchhausen used to tell the story of how he came out of a swamp by pulling himself up by the hair. Thus, Münchhausen-like, we have sporadically tried to pull ourselves out of what is obviously also our condition, imagining ourselves as *not* animals. Whence this desire to elevate ourselves above the cycle of nature in the first place? Is the clean, technological, plastic-and-steel life-style shaping us into beings who try to avoid any contact with

The worst environmental catastrophe to date occurred 24 March 1989, when the oil tanker Exxon Valdez ran aground in Prince William Sound, Alaska. More than 10 million gallons of raw oil polluted almost 1,200 miles of coastal areas, destroying fish, fowl, and marine animals. It is improbable that the wildlife variation and abundance of the area will ever be reestablished. (IFOT)

the steaming bowels of biological reality? Is this why urbanites are so repulsed by fish slime and animal blood? Why may the visitors to the zoo not see the lions being fed with living food? Why are children nowadays taught to use the Latin *orca* instead of the time-honored and perfectly precise *killer whale*? Is it hypocrisy or blindness? Or are we in the process of developing a subspecies of humans who are able to manage emotions only by turning their backs on the realities of life, because they are perceived to be indelicate or repulsive?

The skinning of a lynx, trapped in the woods and still warm after the kill, the flensing of a bowhead whale on a beautiful pebble beach, the harpooning of a ringed seal in its breathing hole in the ice— these are all simply too close to the realities of nature to be palatable. The very thought of such violence makes people dizzy, and they don't know how to handle it. There is nothing easier for a skilled campaign team, then, than to make good business out of turning people against those loathsome animal killers and trying to pull them

Preparing to pack out caribou. Arctic Village, Alaska. (Photo by Richard A. Caulfield, Fairbanks, Alaska)

out of their bloody business by their hair: stop them! destroy their markets, vilify them, criminalize them!

One day, the inanity of this entire exercise is bound to appear. We humans cannot elevate ourselves above the basic realities of nature, and the more we try to repress death and suffering in our view of nature as we would like it to be, the more insidiously death and cruelty will creep into our own day-to-day existence and take us from behind. The fact is there, staring us in the face: the technological-industrial population centers, with their hygienic and clean-cut life-style, with their nature-protection societies and animal-rights campaigns, teem with violence and murder. Those are the places where you look over your shoulder when you go for a walk in the park.

Animal killing in itself certainly does not condition people to bloodthirsty or cruel behavior. Until a generation ago, the private butchering of pigs and cows was commonplace in the back yards of thousands of farms all over Europe and North America. But nobody has ever contended that the two world wars were started in order to gratify the bloodthirst of farm boys from Germany, France, or the American Midwest.

In the Faroe Islands, so decried for their communal pilot whale hunt, the butchering of whales and the inevitable blood in the water are viewed calmly by every child and grown-up. Yet to this day, the Faroes have a virtually crime- and violence-free society.

Nature is not cute. Nobody can try to promote a "Bambification" of its creatures and go unpunished. The built-in need to kill and feed on fellow creatures is as real an aspect of life as romance. Both aspects demand acceptance and respect.

Heading Where?

There are those who claim that the future of humankind lies in vegetarianism. This idea is put forth on the basis of calculations about how many pounds of vegetable fodder have to be used in order to produce one pound of pork or beef, in conjunction with estimates of the world population's growth and resources.[13] But this idea is also defended on ethical grounds, with the argument that it will soon be looked upon as immoral to eat meat.[14] One could claim that we have already taken a step in that direction when it has become possible to get almost an entire nation not to wear fur, as is the case in England.

Will *Homo sapiens*, the animal killer, the omnivore, in some distant future evolve into a calm and sedate vegetarian? That truly would be a sensational development, and there are no convincing arguments to that effect.

For one thing, there are no indications how life in the Arctic could ever be upheld on a vegetarian diet. Vegetables cannot be grown in the Arctic to any meaningful extent. Moreover, the number of calories needed for fitness and physical performance in subzero temperatures is such that meat and animal fat are mandatory as the mainstays of the daily diet, the consumption of sea mammals being the most beneficial.

If we are to take our scientific advisers seriously, general pollution by heavy metals, pesticides, PCBs, and dioxin will assume dangerous levels in the years to come. Unless very quick and extensive structural changes are effectuated in the polluting industries around the world, the accumulation of these contaminants in the polar food chain may cause all the Arctic animals of prey to become extinct by a slow but certain loss of their reproductive ability. The polar bear and the killer whale would be the first victims, maybe as early as fifty years from now. After that it would be the walruses, the seals, and the toothed whales. The closer the animals are to the top of the food chain, the more serious is the problem. We also cannot afford to ignore completely the warnings from some specialists that in a matter of a few generations, surviving sea mammals may simply become so polluted that they will be unfit for human consumption.[15]

Whether these doomsday visions will become reality only time can show. For our purposes, though, it makes no sense to try to build a revolutionary new ethic on potential future catastrophes. For us, the fact remains that only a meat-eater can live in symbiosis with Arctic nature.

Public debate between animal-rights vegetarians on the one hand and inveterate meat-eaters on the other has grown emotional and acrimonious. But we would do well to remember that, on average, we are all normal people with common sense and a responsible attitude toward life. We have our different backgrounds and different value judgments, and we all have a right to be here. The Hindus of India have never attempted to push a don't-eat-beef attitude on the Western societies, promoting their cult of the holy cow, and it surely would be ill taken if they tried. In the Arctic communities, it is taken just as badly when somebody from Toronto, Melbourne, or Am-

Brotherhood: "Do you absolutely have to eat dead animals? Can't you just eat hamburgers like the rest of us?" (During preparations for the 1991 Whaling Commission meeting, differences arose between the Faroese and the Danish Social Democrats. In the cartoon, a political leader from Denmark addresses the Faroe Islands premier, who is sitting at the table, whale meat on his plate.) (Drawing by Óli Petersen, Sosialurin, Tórshavn, Faroe Islands)

sterdam tries to push a don't-eat-seal-or-whale attitude onto those whose whole life is interwoven with precisely that eating habit. Different peoples, different climates, different diets. Different cultures, different emotions. In a shrinking world, we all have to find a way to share the planet.

Without a doubt, the Creator had good reason to endow each of us with only one mouth but two ears: as always, it is important to listen and to understand before we speak. Moreover, the brain that lies between those two ears has been given the ability of recollection: we must never forget whence we came and must always remember that whether our opponent is called Jacob or Esau, he is our twin brother whom we cannot destroy without harming ourselves.

Where are we heading, then?

Maybe the World Conservation Strategy of 1991 affords us the clue. Issued by such authoritative organizations as the World Conservation Union, the United Nations Environment Programme and the World Wide Fund for Nature, this document indicates a course plotted by an impressive array of the world's best experts on matters of the environment and development. Significantly, the document has been given the title *Caring for the Earth*. It is no longer sufficient just to coolly mastermind a strategy. We have to bring our emotions to bear on the issue, making it a matter not only for our heads but for our hearts as well. Saving a livable planet for our grandchildren seems an overwhelming task. It takes everything we can give: we must *care*. Consequently this document takes a new and holistic approach, aiming at a global ethic of conservation and development and calling for cultural and religious leaders as much as for politicians to set the course.

The authors of *Caring for the Earth* are in no doubt that the 200 million indigenous peoples of the earth[16] must be drawn into the decision-making process, together with policy makers, development planners, and conservation scientists and managers. Attention must be paid to the informal yet very practical and useful knowledge about nature stored in the traditions of those who still make a living from wildlife harvest. The aboriginal rights of these peoples to their lands and resources must be formally recognized, including the right to harvest the animals on which their ways of life depend. The dominant societies must cease to hold paternalistic attitudes: people in the bush are also people! Have no doubt about it: this is a call to the very many governments around the world that have solid traditions of just the opposite attitude.

On the issue of wild resources harvest, *Caring for the Earth* tells us that local needs should have priority over external commercial and recreational uses.[17] This surely is a message for Alaska, among other places.

The fur trade conflict between animal-rights proponents and the indigenous peoples of North America and Greenland is noted in this document with the comment that "ethical principles need to be developed to resolve these dilemmas."[18] The dominant species' moral obligation to ensure the involvement of wildlife hunters in formulating these ethical principles is in itself one such principle, forestalling as it does the simple elimination of wildlife harvest that is so ardently sought by some.

The *World Conservation Strategy* of 1980, the Brundtland Commission Report of 1987, and *Caring for the Earth* of 1991 all let us know that time is up. We are told that if we don't set the right course *now*, the basic ecological world order will suffer such damage as has never

Eskimo blanket toss during the summer whaling festival. Kaktovik, Alaska. (Photo by Richard A. Caulfield, Fairbanks, Alaska)

been seen before, and humankind will have to pay a price the full extent of which nobody can anticipate.

There are solid reasons to be deeply concerned, but pessimists are of no use. The way to deal with negative people is to "cut them right in the middle of their litanies and give them work to do." "Pessimism stems from a sense of hopelessness and helplessness, and human beings have never been helpless. . . . Given a transcendent vision, people have proved themselves capable of uniting across their differences . . . when it is clear that their destinies are interlocked."[19]

Our destinies are interlocked, and of course we are capable of reaching across our differences.

All we need is to *want* to reach out, intensely, and then do it.

Notes

Chapter 2. The Seal War

1. Chapter 2 is based generally on Herscovici, *Second Nature*; Henke, *Seal Wars*; and Kapel, "Trends in Catches of Harp and Hooded Seals in Greenland, 1939–83," and *"Phoca groenlandica Erxleben, 1777."* Both of Kapel's works include extensive bibliographies concerning the hunt on harp seals. A further important source is the report from the so-called Malouf Commission set up by the Canadian government with the mandate to examine thoroughly the controversy surrounding the seal hunt. The report is called *Seals and Sealing in Canada.*

2. Quoted in Herscovici, *Second Nature*, p. 74.

3. This attempt succeeded in 1968.

4. Johansen, *Krop og Klaer*, pp. 98–100 (Marianne Stenbaek's translation).

5. Egede, *A Description of Greenland*, p. 102.

6. Alice Miller, in her book *For Your Own Good*, does not deal with the baby seal issue, of course. But her observations are well in line with this reasoning. According to Miller, Western civilization has about the worst record of child abuse in history, and it has left in the subconscious of many people deep scars of guilt and fear, feelings crying out for compensation. See also Herscovici, *Second Nature*, p. 95.

7. Concerning the interests of the North American organizations, see Herscovici, *Second Nature*, pp. 70, 218, 227, 228.

8. "Live aus dem Schlachthof," television debate broadcast on Bayrische Rundfunk, Munich, 15 January 1990 (author's translation; videotape copy in the author's file).

9. Gifford et al., "Inside the Environmental Groups," pp. 69–84.

10. The European Council's Directive 83/129/EEC about the import into member states of certain kinds of seal pelts and goods fashioned thereof took effect on 1 October 1983, at first for two years and then for another four years. Finally in 1989 it went into effect for an unlimited time period. The directive prohibits imports and trade in the European Common Market of fur from whitecoats and blueblacks, that is, the pups of harp and hooded seals.

In art. 3 the directive makes an exception for goods derived from "the traditional hunt carried out by the Inuit populations"—a free gift from the European Common Market to Greenland, northern Quebec, and the Northwest Territories in Canada. This has no impact at all and does not cost the EEC anything, since the Inuit do not carry out a commercial seal pup hunt anyway. The European Common Market's preferential treatment of the Inuit consists solely in distinguishing them, and in a positive way, from other seal hunters.

11. *Greenland Seals.*

12. In 1985, Greenpeace and Indigenous Survival International (ISI) agreed to start a dialogue about the sealskin market. A summer trip to the Uummannaq district in northern Greenland was arranged. Greenpeace in England sent Alan Pickaver and Lorraine Thorne. In addition to representatives from ISI, Tommy Dybbroe from the WWF in Denmark participated.

On 31 August a public meeting was held with the population in the small settlement of Niaqornat. Pickaver offered an official apology on behalf of Greenpeace for the unintentional harm that the campaign against the seal pup hunt near Newfoundland had caused the Inuit; he further expressed the hope that the Arctic hunting communities and Greenpeace could work together so that such detrimental effects could be avoided in the future.

The meeting was taped in its entirety by Denmark's national television, and the apology by Pickaver was shown on the Danish television news. Pickaver wrote a confidential report to the Greenpeace headquarters about the group's experiences: "Report on the Greenpeace Meeting with Indigenous Survival International, Greenland, August 30–September 2, 1985." Appendix 3 of the report contains the description of the meeting in Niaqornat and Pickaver's own formulation of the apology to the seal hunters (on file at Arctic Information, Montergade 16, Copenhagen).

Chapter 3. The Whale War

1. Egede, *A Description of Greenland*, chap. 7; Nelson, *Make Prayers to the Raven*.

2. *Our Way of Whaling*, p. 29. This is a translation of the original Danish text in Knud Rasmussen, *Festens Gave* (Gyldendal, Copenhagen, 1929).

3. ICES-F, "6. Report of the North-Western Working Group."

4. On 30 January 1990 the general secretary of the ICES asked the members of the working group concerning the North Atlantic salmon, the North Atlantic Salmon Convention (NASCO), to make sure that their work was not "corrupted" by national political concerns. The general secretary emphasized the fine tradition of the ICES, going back as far as 1902, for independent scientific work, and he further expressed the wish that the political problems which might be raised in NASCO not be brought forward to the ICES to degrade the work carried out there.

5. "The oceanic feeling" is one of the main themes in the writings of the American psychiatrist Stanislav Grof. His *Journeys beyond the Brain* contains illustrations of experiences of oceanic ecstasies.

6. I have based this paragraph on various comments by representatives from the WWF and Greenpeace during a public hearing arranged by the International Work Group for Indigenous Affairs (IWGIA) on Arctic resources and environmental strategies. The hearing took place in the Danish parliament building in Copenhagen, 27 September 1988 (audiotape on file at Arctic Information, Montergade 16, Copenhagen).

7. Franz, *The Process of Individuation*, in the book edited by Carl G. Jung and M.-L. von Franz, *Man and His Symbols*, part 3, pp. 158−229.

8. In 1982 the IWC decided to stop all commercial whaling from 1986 until the end of 1990. It was originally the idea that the IWC during these five years would undertake an assessment of the stocks of all the various whale species it dealt with, in order to decide, before 1991, whether and to what extent commercial whaling could be reinstituted. But the IWC has been able to assess only some of the stocks, and no commercial whaling has been resumed.

9. Aboriginal subsistence whaling means whaling, for purposes of local consumption carried out by or on behalf of aboriginal, indigenous or native peoples who share strong community, familial, social and cultural ties related to a continuing traditional dependence on whaling and on the use of whales.

Local aboriginal consumption means the traditional uses of whale products by local, aboriginal, indigenous or native communities in meeting their nutritional, subsistence and cultural requirements. The term includes trade in items which are by-products of subsistence catches.

Subsistence catches are catches of whales by aboriginal subsistence whaling operations. (IWC doc. 40/5)

Three broad objectives for the management of aboriginal subsistence whaling were accepted by the IWC in 1981:

To ensure that the risks of extinction to individual stocks are not seriously increased by subsistence whaling;

To enable aboriginal people to harvest whales in perpetuity at levels appropriate to their cultural and nutritional requirements, subject to the other objectives;

To maintain the status of whale stocks at or above the level giving the highest net recruitment and to ensure that stocks below that level are moved towards it, so far as the environment permits. (IWC report, special issue 4, p. 84)

10. For the summary that follows here, I have relied on Gad, *The History of Greenland*.

11. Josefsen, *Cutter Hunting of Minke Whale in Qaqortoq (Greenland)*, p. 17.

12. Dahl, "Hunting and Subsistence in Greenland in the Light of Socio-Economic Relations"; Petersen, "Traditional and Present Distribution Channels in Subsistence Hunting in Greenland"; Caulfield, *Qeqertarsuarmi arfanniarneq*, pp. 7−8.

13. And rightly so. The campaign against the exploitation of sea mammals is in contradiction to human rights as they are expressed in two international covenants signed on 16 December 1966, one concerned with economic, social, and cultural rights and the other with civil and political rights. Both of these covenants state in chap. 1, art. 1, no. 2, that "all peoples may,

for their own ends, freely dispose of their natural wealth and resources. . . . In no case may a people be deprived of its own means of subsistence." These covenants have been signed by all the countries that stand behind the anti-whaling campaigns.

14. Singer, *Animal Liberation*. He argues that no such experiment can be justifiable at all "unless [it] is so important that the use of a retarded human being would also be justifiable" (Avon ed., p. 78).

15. At this point, it might be objected that in the human realm, also, we have important instances where rights are dissociated from duties. One obvious example is the human predicament of helplessness at the beginning and at the end of life. Infants enjoy the protection of human rights but have no duties. The same thing goes for the senile elderly. We conclude that it *is* possible, in some cases even right and proper, to dissociate rights from duties. Duties furthermore appear as a narrower concept than rights. But if we can accept rights without duties in humans, then perhaps we should also accept the disjunction in whales.

Nobody, though, can deny that the state of an infant or of a senile person represents the exception to the rule, which is the intimate association of rights and duties characteristic of *responsibility*. The human person is essentially *the responsible animal*, which experiences first an ascent and later a decline of the capacity for responsibility. This ascent and decline of maturity, with its blurring or suspension of the duties aspect of the moral power, is part of the whole, the characteristic of which clearly is an *accountability*, which is unique to *Homo sapiens*. In the human person, we can accept instances of rights without duties because these instances are integrated and natural parts of a whole, the main feature of which is rights *with* duties. The infant and the senile person have their human rights because they are going to exercise, or have exercised, a kind of accountability that no other animal is capable of showing at any point of its life-span.

The case of the mentally ill or retarded person is not much different. It is true that there are many persons who are given dispensations from the otherwise normal duties of life, while retaining some basic and inalienable rights, such as the right to life and to living conditions as decent as their circumstances make possible. However, the attempt to define a set of properties in a healthy and normal population of one species on the basis of the properties inherent in sick individuals of a completely different species brings the matter to a point where the rationale of the argument is hard to take seriously.

16. Barstow, "Beyond Whale Species Survival," pp. 10–13. Barstow is American. The official New Zealand position in the whaling issue points in the same direction. At the third session of the preparatory committee of the UN Conference on Environment and Development, the New Zealand delegate stated that whales are "in a sense the equivalent in the marine environment of human beings in the land environment" (UNCED Prep. Com., Working Group II, Geneva, 12 August 1991, item 2, "Statement on Cetaceans," p. 12).

17. D'Amato and Chopra, "Whales," p. 61.

18. According to the Scientific Committee of the IWC, the Bering-

Chukchi-Beaufort Seas stock of bowhead whales numbers around 8,000 animals and is growing. The scientists operate with a "lower bound" and a "most probable" estimate. For 1991 the two figures are 6,785 and 8,171. For 1994 the "most probable" estimate is 8,801. The probable growth of the stock, then, is several hundred animals per year. The lower bound for the growth is 92 animals per year. The Alaska Eskimo quota is 54 animals struck or 41 landed, whichever of the two is attained first, a figure that represents a fraction of the probable growth of the stock (IWC doc. 43/4 no. 7.1, *Bering-Chukchi-Beaufort Seas Stock of Bowhead Whales: Management Advice*). This is a textbook example of a sustainable wildlife harvest.

19. The factory-ship moratorium dates back to 1980. In actual fact, it has more the character of a ban (IWC Schedule art. 10 [d]).

20. Canada left the IWC in 1982. In 1991, Iceland announced its intention to do the same thing in 1992.

21. Brundtland Commission, *Our Common Future*, chapter subsection entitled "Empowering Vulnerable Groups." See also the International Labor Organization (ILO) Convention, doc. no. 169, on indigenous and tribal peoples' rights.

As a follow-up to the Brundtland Commission's work, UNEP held a conference in New York in 1987 in cooperation with the multinational company Ciba-Geigy. The objective was to further the interest among businessmen in a sustainable utilization of natural resources. This quotation comes from the conference report, *Only One Earth Forum*, p. 88:

2. Respect for Traditional Practices.
Nature conservation and management practices should take into account not only attitudes and policies developed in academia and higher levels of administration, but grassroots traditional attitudes as well. Much accumulated, nonformalized wisdom is to be found among the actual users of the natural environment, especially among Fourth World population groups (defined as the indigenous peoples of the world who, living on the land of their ancestors and upholding their traditional values, are dominated by subsequent technologically and numerically stronger nations). Fauna, fowl and fish, lands, wetlands, rivers, and other bodies of water already in use and already being managed in various ways should be subjected to new conservation measures by the dominant society only in collaboration with those living on the land, and with respect for the traditional management practices already developed by them.

3. Harvest of Wildlife.
Primordial human lifestyles, in which daily food is taken directly from the surrounding wild vegetation and wildlife, are still observed in important areas of all five continents. Stocks of fish, fowl, and fauna in the wild, harvested on a sustainable-yield basis, represent valuable and often indispensable food resources for numerous population groups around the world who, in many ways, have been dispossessed of formal title to their ancestral lands.
This tradition of food procurement, which is basic to the livelihood of these peoples, is being threatened in several ways: (a) habitat destruction; (b) unfairly restrictive legislation; (c) erosion of traditional conservation practices; and (d) destruction of markets for the products of these groups.
In cases where traditional food procurement from the wild is being obstructed or eliminated, the need for nutritional replacement values is seldom taken into account.

The result is frequently malnutrition and unnecessary associated health problems among the indigenous peoples.

Development projects and legislation touching upon indigenous hunting and fishing rights should be planned and implemented in close consultation with the local populations, in a manner that will not adversely affect their food procurement opportunities.

Dominant societies should accept the responsibility of securing, through appropriate legislative measures, a market for products originating from aboriginal subsistence economies.

Chapter 4. *The Battle of the Traps*

1. *Times* (London), 21 December 1988: "Animal rights activists claim store attacks." The terrorist bomb attacks were mentioned in many British newspapers around 21 December and in the days following.

2. *Daily Star*, 19 December 1984: "We don't care if people die."

3. *Guardian*, 20 December 1984: "Animal rights 'psychotics' condemned on all sides of House."

4. *Daily Express*, 24 February 1989: "Police hunt fanatics as Animal Lib extremists warn: Next time we kill. Silence of the scientists in fear."

5. *Times* (London), 24 February 1989: "Animal madhouse."

6. *Times* (London), May 1985: "Animal rights: the painful decisions."

7. See note 3 to this chapter.

8. Cherfas, "Two Bomb Attacks on Scientists in the U.K.," p. 1485.

9. "Tierversuchsgegener Hessen e. V.," 11 December 1989: "Gnädige Frau—wie hätten Sie denn gern Ihren Pelz?"

10. "Institut fur Gesellschaftswissenschaften Walberberg e. V. Pressemitteilung," 11 December 1989: "10 Thesen von P. Dr. Heinrich Basilius Streithofen." *Weser-Kurier*, 18 December 1989: "Tierschutzer drohen mit Austritt aus der Kirche." The Danish magazine *Forsoegsdyrenes Vaern*, no. 1, 1990, carries a press release from the World Council of Churches which states that Christians ought not to buy furs.

11. Canada, House of Commons, Standing Committee on Aboriginal Affairs and Northern Development, *The Fur Issue*.

12. Written declaration by Barbara Castle and Madron Seligman about traps, European Parliament, 15 June 1988, PE 124.655.

13. Proposal for a council regulation (EEC) on the importation of certain furs, Commission of the European Communities, 26 April 1989, Com (89) 198 final.

14. Telephone conversation with the chairman of the ISO-TC 191, Neal Jotham, in Ottawa, 28 May 1990.

15. Chairman's report on the development of international humane trapping standards, Secretariat of the ISO/TC 191, 17 November 1989, "Trapping Research: Brief Summary of Progress to Date"; information supplied by Environment Canada and the FIC, November 1989.

16. Hannah Maij-Weggen, draft report on the proposal for a council regulation (EEC) on the importation of certain furs (COM [89] 198 final-

doc. C3-82/89), European Parliament, 11 October 1989, PE 134.347, minutes from the European Parliament's Committee for External Economic Relations, Brussels, 10 November 1989; Mrs. Maria A. Agliettas' report to the Committee for External Economic Relations, 16 November 1989, PE 136.20; amendments to the Caroline Jackson report on the leg-hold trap of August 1988 (PE 126.039) (Madron Seligman, Seibel Emmeling, et al.); Mrs. Flathers, preliminary draft opinion of the Section for Protection of the Environment, Public Health and Consumer Affairs on the proposal for a council regulation (EEC) on the importation of certain furs (COM [89] 198 final), European Communities Economic and Social Committee, Brussels, 11 September 1989; Mary Banotti, proposal by the Committee for Environmental and Health Concerns and Consumer Protection concerning the European Commission's proposal to the council's document on the import of certain furs, European Parliament meeting document A3-0138/90, 7 June 1990. Complete documentation of the very extensive debate can be obtained from the European Parliament's Environmental and Consumer Protection Committee secretariat in Brussels.

17. *Sunday Telegraph*, 29 October 1989: "Death sentence for furs."
18. The press release reads as follows: "As naive as it may sound, our sponsorship and participation in the Lynx Fashion Show was not intended to be more than an effort to sell more product. In future, Gore, as a company, will NOT align itself with Lynx or any other special interest groups" (*International Fur Trade Federation News* [20/21 Queenhithe, London], no. 2, June 1990).
19. *Fishing News International*, August 1989: "Junk food for a whale."
20. Spillius et al., "Environmental Costs of Synthetic Versus Natural Mink Furs."
21. Jensen, "Report on Organochlorines," in *Arctic Centre Publications 2*, 1991, pp. 335–384; *Toronto Globe and Mail*, 21 December 1988: "Chemical pollution from USSR, Europe found in Arctic food chain."

Chapter 5. Which Way?

1. Harris, *Cannibals and Kings*, chap. 3.
2. Gen. 25: 23, King James Version.
3. The dominant society's attitude toward the indigenous peoples who are under its control often displays an appalling insensitivity to cultural factors. An example of this kind of blind spot is in the contributions by the vice-president of the International Wildlife Coalition (Toronto, Canada), Stephen Best, to a hearing arranged by the Canadian Arctic Resources Committee (CARC) at the Centre for Northern Studies and Research, McGill University, in Montreal (*A Question of Rights*, pp. 138–44).
The IWGIA, with headquarters at Fiolstraede 10, Copenhagen K, Denmark, (telephone 45-33 12 47 24), has extensive material on file about the repression of indigenous peoples throughout the world.
4. For more on this strategy, see "Heading Where?" at the end of this chapter.

The conflict between the concepts of "wise use" and "no use" of nature and their respective influence on contemporary American legislation are analyzed in Manning, *Marine Mammals and Fisheries Conflict*. The idea of "wise use" of nature was given its first formal hearing in the United States by President Theodore Roosevelt, who himself was a big-game hunter. As a cofounder of the Boone and Crocket Club around the turn of the century, he started a wildlife-management system that formed the basis of the management regimes of the big national parks in the United States in the first part of this century. After the Second World War, the idea spread that national parks are better served by letting protected nature look after itself and that people, or at least hunters, should be kept out. Especially in the English-speaking part of the world, the idea has gained prominence that, by and large, nature is best served by not using it and that any use of wild nature is detrimental to the ecological balance. This kind of thinking leads directly to an antagonistic attitude toward the aboriginal hunters' and gatherers' life-style and creates a "no-use" sentiment that opposes any use of animals.

5. Peter Armitage, "Low-Level Military Flights and the Destruction of Innu Culture," *IWGIA Newsletter*, no. 45, 1986, pp. 43–62; The Innu Nation, "An Open Letter to the People of Great Britain, the Netherlands and West Germany from the Innu Nation," Airbase Camp, Ntesian, 12 October 1988 (on file at IWGIA, Copenhagen); North Atlantic Peace Organization (NAPO), "NATO in Labrador/Québec," updates no. 5, March 1989, and no. 6, Fall 1989; Judy Rowell, "Northern Labrador's Biggest Developer: The Department of National Defence," and Hon. Bill Rompkey, MP, and Brig. Gen. C. D. Young, "Northern Perspectives Interviews," *Northern Perspectives* (CARC), vol. 18, no. 2, March–April 1990, pp. 11–20.

6. Komarov, *The Destruction of Nature in the Soviet Union*; Chichlo, *Current Problems of the Indigenous Peoples of Siberia*, "Les Nevuqaghmiit ou la fin d'une ethnie," *Études/Inuit/Studies* (Université Laval, Quebec), vol. 5, no. 2, 1989; Vladimir Lupandin and Yevdokia Gayer, "Chernobyl on the Chukot Peninsula," *Moscow News*, no. 34, 1989, p. 5.

7. Many resolutions concerned with these problems have been passed at general assemblies both in the ICC and in ISI. The resolutions can be obtained at the following addresses:

Inuit Circumpolar Conference
170 Laurier Avenue West
Ottawa, Ontario K1P 5V5
Canada   (telephone 1–613–563–2642)

Indigenous Survival International
298 Elgin Street, Suite 105
Ottawa, Ontario K2P 1M3
Canada   (telephone 1–613–230–3616)

8. Balikci, "Anthropology, film and the Arctic peoples."
9. Quoted in Balikci, "Anthropology," p. 6.

10. Isa. 11: 6–7, King James Version.
11. Singer, *Animal Liberation*, English ed. p. 252, footnote.
12. Council for Yukon Indians; *Our Land Our Culture Our Future.*
13. Singer, *Animal Liberation*, English ed., pp. 178–179.
14. Singer, *Animal Liberation*, English ed., p. 250 and passim.
According to Singer, the problem comes from widespread and accepted "speciesism," according to which human beings automatically put their own frivolous and inane preferences over the vital interests of animals, as if human beings were superior. Morally, he argues, speciesism is just as reprehensible as racism or male chauvinism. From this point of view, vegetarianism becomes a moral imperative, especially since eating meat and, hence, killing animals are no longer necessary.

The thoughts of Peter Singer have attracted much attention in the English-speaking world. In our context the best document to consult might be *A Question of Rights*, which includes an essay by Anne Doncaster of the Toronto Humane Society, much inspired by the Singer concept of animal liberation.

Singer himself does not draw the same conclusions from his premises as do the animal-rights people in Toronto (such as Anne Doncaster and Stephen Best, see note no. 3, p. 109). In 1987 he said in an interview with the American periodical *Animal's Agenda* (vol. 7, no. 7, p. 8):

I think basically that we ought to stay away from those areas where we're coming into conflict with people who really have a survival need or a very deep cultural need. I think it's a mistake for environmentalists and animal liberationists to focus on the Eskimo killings of bowhead whales when there is so much more whale killing done by the Japanese. In think that if the killing is indeed either necessary for their survival or a central part of their culture, then it just doesn't seem appropriate for us, given the incredible scale of abuse that Western society has inflicted on animals, to rush over to Alaska, and say, "Hey, you people are killing 50 whales a year (or whatever) and you've got to stop that." Maybe when we've cleaned up our own act, then we could start to look at what other people are doing. If the native people are killing animals as part of a traditional way of life, I think we really can't rightfully interfere.

Later in the same text, Singer also states that a commercialization of the aboriginal peoples' resource utilization would change the picture.

15. Comité Arctique International at its symposium in Oslo, September 1989. To date the minutes have not been published, but I have had discussions with the participants Dr. David Kinloch, the chief of the Field Epidemiology Division in the Canadian Department of Health and Welfare (in Rovaniemi, Finland, 25 September 1989), and the scientific liaison officer, Joergen Taagholt, from the Danish Polar Center (Copenhagen, 1 April 1990).

16. *Caring for the Earth*, p. 61, box 11.
17. P. 41, action 4.13.
18. P. 15, box 3.
19. The first quotation comes from Muller, *Most of All, They Taught Me Happiness*, p. 173, and the second from Norman Cousins's Foreword to Muller's book, p. 9.

Bibliography

Arctic Centre Publications, 2. The State of the Arctic Environment Reports. Arctic Centre, University of Lapland. Rovaniemi, Finland. 1991.

Aron, William: "The Commons Revisited: Thoughts on Marine Mammal Management." *Coastal Management.* Vol. 16, 1988, pp. 99–110.

Balikci, Asen: "Anthropology, Film and the Arctic Peoples: The First Forman Lecture." *Anthropology Today.* Vol. 5, no. 2, April 1989, pp. 4–10.

Barstow, Robbins: "Beyond Whale Species Survival." *Sonar. The Magazine of the Whale and Dolphin Society.* No. 2, Autumn 1989, pp. 10–13.

Bonner, W. Nigel: *Whales.* Blandford Press. Pool & Dorset, U.K. 1980.

Brody, Hugh: *Living Arctic: Hunters of the Canadian North.* Faber & Faber. London & Boston. 1987.

Campbell, Joseph: *The Way of the Animal Powers.* Historical Atlas of World Mythology. Vol. 1. Alfred Van Der Marck Editions. Harper & Row. San Francisco. 1983.

Canada. House of Commons, Ottawa, Standing Committee on Aboriginal Affairs and Northern Development: *The Fur Issue: Cultural Continuity, Economic opportunity.* 1986.

Canada. Indian and Northern Affairs, Ottawa: *State of the Arctic Environment: Report on Chlorinated Organics, Executive Summary.* 1990.

Caring for the Earth. IUCN. Gland, Switzerland. 1991.

Caulfield, Richard A.: *Qeqertarsuarmi arfanniarneq: Greenlandic Inuit Whaling in Qeqertarsuaq Kommune, West Greenland.* Department of Rural Development, University of Alaska. Fairbanks. 1991.

Cherfas, Jeremy: "Two Bomb Attacks on Scientists in the U.K." *Science,* Vol. 248, 22 June 1990, p. 1485.

Chichlo, Boris: *Current Problems of the Indigenous Peoples of Siberia.* IMSECO. Paris. 1989.

Council for the Yukon Indians: *Our Land Our Culture Our Future.* N.p. N.d.

Cummins, Joseph E.: "Extinction: The PCB Threat to Marine Mammals." *Ecologist.* Vol. 18, no. 6, 1988, pp. 193–95.

Dahl, Jens: "Hunting and Subsistence in Greenland in the Light of Socio-

Economic Relations." In *Greenland Subsistence Hunting*, IWC doc. 41/22. Chap. 4. 1989.

D'Amato, Anthony, and Sudhir K. Chopra: "Whales: Their Emerging Right to Life." *American Journal of International Law*. Vol. 85, no. 1, January 1991, pp. 21–62.

Dubos, René: *Celebrations of Life*. McGraw-Hill Book Co. New York. 1981.

Egede, Hans: *A Description of Greenland, with an Historical Introduction and a Life of the Author*. T. and J. Allman. London. 1818.

Environmental Investigation Agency: *The Global War against Small Cetaceans*. London. 1990.

Environmental Investigation Agency: *The Global War against Small Cetaceans*. London. 1991.

Gad, Finn: *The History of Greenland*. 3 vols. Vols. 1–2: C. Hurst. London. 1970, 1973. Vol. 3: Nyt Nordisk Forlag Arnold Busck. Copenhagen. 1982.

Gifford, Bill, et al.: "Inside the Environmental Groups." *Outside*. September 1990.

Greenland Home Rule Authority: *Our Way of Whaling—Arfanniariaaserput*. Nuuk, Greenland. 1988.

Grof, Stanislav: *Beyond the Brain*. State University of New York Press. 1985.

Harris, Marvin: *Cannibals and Kings*. Random House. New York. 1977.

Henke, Janice Scott: *Seal Wars*. Breakwater. St. John's, Newfoundland. 1985.

Henshaw, David: *Animal Warfare: The Story of the Animal Liberation Front*. Fontana/Collins. London. 1990.

Herscovici, Alan: *Second Nature: The Animal-Rights Controversy*. CBC Enterprises. Montreal & Toronto. 1985. 2nd ed. Stoddart Publishing. Toronto. 1991.

———: *Furs—an Environmental Ethic*. J. Theilade. Virum, Denmark. 1988.

Home Rule Informations Service Tusarliivik: *Greenland Seals*. Nuuk, Greenland. 1983.

ICES-F: "6. Report of the North-Western Working Group." 8–12 March 1976.

IWC: *Greenland Subsistence Hunting*. IWC doc. 41/22. 1989.

Johansen, R. Broby: *Krop og Klaer*. Gyldendal. Copenhagen. 1987.

Josefsen, Erling: *Cutter Hunting of Minke Whales in Qaqortoq (Greenland): Case Study*. Greenland Home Rule Government. IWC doc. TC/42 SEST 5. 1990.

Jotham, Neal: *International Humane Trapping Standards Backgrounder, Secretariat of ISO/TC 191: Humane Animal Traps*. Canadian General Standards Board. Ottawa. July 1991.

Jung, Carl G. and Franz, M.-L. von (eds.): *Man and His Symbols*. Doubleday. New York. 1964.

Kapel, Finn: "Trends in Catches of Harp and Hooded Seals in Greenland, 1939–83." *NAFO Scientific Council Studies*, Vol. 10, 1986, pp. 57–65.

———: *"Phoca groenlandica Erxleben, 1777"* (manuscript). 1987.

Klinowska, Margaret: *Dolphins, Porpoises and Whales of the World: The IUCN Red Data Book*. IUCN. Gland, Switzerland, & Cambridge, U.K. 1991.

Komarov, Boris: *The Destruction of Nature in the Soviet Union*. E. M. Sharpe. White Plains. 1980.

Malouf Commission: *Seals and Sealing in Canada*. Report of the Royal Commission. Vols. 1–3. Minister of Supply and Services Canada. Ottawa. 1986.

Manning, Laura L.: "Marine Mammals and Fisheries Conflict: A Philosophical Dispute." *Ocean and Shoreline Management* 12, pp. 217–232. Elsevier Science Publishers. London. 1989.

Mihalisko, Kathleen: "SOS for Native Peoples of Soviet North." *Radio Liberty: Report on the USSR*. Vol. 1, no. 5, February 1989, pp. 3–6.

Miller, Alice: *For Your Own Good*. Farrar, Straus & Giroux. New York. 1984.

Muller, Robert: *Most of All, They Taught Me Happiness*. Image Books. Garden City, N.Y. 1985.

Nelson, Richard: *Make Prayers to the Raven*. University of Chicago Press. Chicago. 1983.

Only One Earth Forum. Proceedings co-sponsored by UNEP and Ciba-Geigy Corporation. The René Dubos Center for Human Environments. New York. 1988.

Petersen, Robert: "Traditional and Present Distribution Channels in Subsistence Hunting in Greenland." In IWC, *Greenland Subsistence Hunting*, IWC doc. 41/22. chap. 5. 1989.

Post, Laurens van der: *A Mantis Carol*. William Morrow & Co., New York. 1976.

A Question of Rights: Northern Wildlife Management and the Anti-Harvest Movement. National Symposium on the North. CARC. Ottawa. 1989.

Regan, Tom: *The Case for Animal Rights*. University of California Press. Berkeley & Los Angeles. 1983.

Regan, Tom, and Peter Singer: *Animal Rights and Human Obligations*. Prentice Hall. Englewood Cliffs, N.J. 2nd ed. 1989.

Restoration Following the Exxon Valdez Oil Spill. Proceedings of the Public Symposium Held in Anchorage, Alaska, 26–27 March 1990. Restoration Planning Work Group. Alaska Departments of Fish and Game, Natural Resources and Environmental Conservation; U.S. Departments of Agriculture, Commerce and Interior: U.S. Environmental Protection Agency. July 1990.

Singer, Peter: *Animal Liberation*. English ed. Thorsons Publishers. Wellingborough, Northamptonshire. 1975. American ed. Avon Books. New York. 1975.

Spillius, J., Learmonth, S., and Leathem, P.: "Environmental Costs of Synthetic Versus Natural Mink Furs: An Evaluation of Arguments." (manuscript). 1977.

Vestergaard, Elisabeth (ed.): *Whaling Communities: Biological Studies; Policy and Regulations; Socio-Cultural Aspects*. North Atlantic Studies, vol. 2, nos. 1 & 2. Aarhus Universitetsforlag. Aarhus, Denmark. 1990.

Watson, Lyall: *Sea Guide to Whales of the World*. E. P. Dutton. New York. 1981.

Wenzel, George: *Animal Rights, Human Rights: Ecology, Economy and Ideology in the Canadian Arctic*. Belhaven Press. London. 1991.

Williamson, R. G.: "Cultural Persistence and Cultural Casualties in the Sealskin Wars." *Proactive*. Vol. 10, no. 1, Spring 1991. p. 16–25.

World Commission on Environment and Development: *Our Common Future*. Oxford University Press. Oxford. 1987.

World Conservation Strategy. IUCN, UNEP, WWF. Gland, Switzerland. 1980.

Index

UNIVERSITY PRESS OF NEW ENGLAND publishes books under its
own imprint and is the publisher for Brandeis University Press, Brown University
Press, University of Connecticut, Dartmouth College, Middlebury College Press,
University of New Hampshire, University of Rhode Island, Tufts University,
University of Vermont, and Wesleyan University Press.

Library of Congress Cataloging-in-Publication Data
Lynge, Finn.
    [Kampen om de vilde dyr. English]
    Arctic wars, animal rights, endangered peoples / Finn Lynge :
translated by Marianne Stenbaek.
        p.   cm.
    Translation of: Kampen om de vilde dyr.
    Includes bibliographical references and index.
    ISBN 0-87451-588-2
    1. Animal rights—Arctic regions.   2. Animals and civilization—
Arctic regions.   3. Hunting—Political aspects—Arctic regions.
4. Indigenous peoples—Arctic regions.   5. Arctic regions—Economic
conditions.   6. Animal rights movement—Europe.   7. Animal rights
movement—Canada.   I. Title.
    HV4890.69.A3L94I3   1992
    179'.3'0998—dc20   92–1516

⊗

Printed in the United States
19914LVS00001B/313-369